As one of the world's longest established
and best-known travel brands,
Thomas Cook are the experts in travel.

For more than 135 years our
guide books have unlocked the secrets
of destinations around the world,
sharing with travellers a wealth of
experience and a passion for travel.

**Rely on Thomas Cook as your
travelling companion on your next trip
and benefit from our unique heritage.**

Thomas Cook **traveller** guides

ISRAEL
Samantha Wilson

D0419903

since 1873

Thomas
Cook

Written by Samantha Wilson
Original photography by Mark Bassett

Published by Thomas Cook Publishing
A division of Thomas Cook Tour Operations Limited
Company registration no. 3772199 England
The Thomas Cook Business Park, Unit 9, Coningsby Road,
Peterborough PE3 8SB, United Kingdom
Email: books@thomascook.com, Tel: +44 (0) 1733 416477
www.thomascookpublishing.com

Produced by Cambridge Publishing Management Limited
Burr Elm Court, Main Street, Caldecote CB23 7NU
www.cambridgepm.co.uk

ISBN: 978-1-84848-478-8

First edition © 2011 Thomas Cook Publishing
Text © Thomas Cook Publishing
Maps © Thomas Cook Publishing/PCGraphics (UK) Limited

Series Editor: Karen Beaulah
Production/DTP: Steven Collins

Printed and bound in Spain by GraphyCems

Cover photography © Michael DeFreitas

Contents

Introduction

Israel is a small country in the Middle East. It is home to profoundly significant religious sites, an eclectic culture, flourishing cities and varied landscapes that range from towering mountains to verdant valleys and arid deserts. Its wealth of tourist appeal is simply enormous and visitors find they leave changed, for the Holy Land touches everyone in some way.

Pilgrims have poured into the Holy Land for centuries, its wealth of religious sites, air of spirituality and undeniable intrigue attracting devotees from far and wide. Today is no different, and Israel is fast becoming one of the most popular new tourist destinations. Yet it isn't just the religious appeal that is drawing the crowds.

Perched on the divide between the northern steppes of Europe and the parched deserts of the south along the great Syrian–African Rift Valley, Israel gets the best of both worlds. The northern region of the Golan Heights and Upper Galilee is characterised by pine forests, gushing waterfalls and high, snow-capped peaks, while the area comprising the central plateau and Lower Galilee has gently rolling lands where agriculture thrives and towns and cities flourish. Israel marks the end of the Mediterranean Sea, and its long coastline has seen centuries of activity. Today, the great cities of Tel Aviv, Haifa and Akko enjoy the warm climate and

sandy beaches, while archaeological sites such as Caesarea have stood the tests of time and reward visitors with unparalleled remains. Inland is Jerusalem, the Holy City, a mere hour from Tel Aviv and the coast. At its core sits the Old City, an intriguing treasure trove that will leave even the most apathetic of visitors in awe.

Forming a whopping half of the country is the desert, where craggy rock mountains and valleys are interspersed with fertile oases and small kibbutzim. At its foot, with views across to Egypt, Jordan and Saudi Arabia, is the Red Sea, its reefs teeming with corals and tropical fish.

The country has had a colourful and turbulent short life, and long before the State of Israel was declared just over six decades ago, the land on which it stands has had an even more colourful past. The remains of ancient civilisations remain in the landscape, the finds unearthed now housed within Israel's world-class museums.

Influxes of immigration have given rise to a deeply diverse and interesting cultural make-up as reflected in the varied languages spoken, cuisines, music styles and theatre. Despite the political troubles so carefully documented by the world's media, Israel is from day to day a peaceful country, where the residents work hard, love their families and enjoy their leisure time, their natural world and socialising.

A trip to Israel is something many dream of, and one which more and more people are realising. It was once a country many were intrigued by but also a place to which travel seemed illogical or even dangerous. Yet today, being just a four-hour flight from Europe, city breaks, family holidays, independent travel and pilgrimages are easier than ever. For Israel is a destination where the answer to 'Do you speak English?' is replied with 'Of course', a place where the calibre of restaurants competes with those of France, and a country which remains unchallenged in its wealth of historical, archaeological and religious sites.

A view of Jerusalem from the Mount of Olives

The land

Measuring 423km (263 miles) from north to south and 114km (71 miles) at its widest point, Israel is a small country but its widely varying landscape ranges from the great deserts of the south to the verdant valleys of the north. Sitting in the vast Syrian–African Rift Valley, it has borders with Lebanon, Syria, Jordan, Egypt and the Palestinian Territories and sits on the crossroads where the continents of Africa and Asia meet.

Geography

Israel is a geographically diverse country. The green, tree-studded north is characterised by snow-capped mountains, rivers and sweeping fertile valleys, the Hermon Mountain (2,224m/7,296ft), 250km (155-mile)-long Jordan River, Jezreel Valley and Sea of Galilee standing out as the most significant natural features. The 270km (167-mile)-long Mediterranean coast is home to major cities such as Tel Aviv, Haifa and Akko, with Jerusalem located inland on the fringes of the huge, arid deserts of the south. In their midst sits the Dead Sea, the earth's lowest point on dry land and a unique geological marvel at 433m (1,420ft) below sea level. At its southernmost tip, Israel meets the Red Sea with a short 14km (8-mile) coastline.

Cities

Israel's capital city is Jerusalem, although for political reasons most countries maintain embassies in Tel Aviv. These two cities, the country's biggest, couldn't in fact be more different. Jerusalem represents the traditional, with centuries-old architecture, devout residents and a profound religious and political history, while Tel Aviv is a young, fun-loving, secular city with sprawling white, sandy beaches and boulevards lined with cafés. The third-largest city is Haifa, further north on the Mediterranean coast and resting on the northern tip of the Mount Carmel range. This relaxed and pleasant city is home to a major port, naval base and big university and is headquarters of the Bahá'í faith.

While Israel has several large cities, most are residential hubs and hold little appeal for visitors. Major exceptions include: Tiberias on the shore of the Sea of Galilee; the holy Jewish city of Tzfat in the Upper Galilee; the predominantly Christian Arab city of Nazareth in the Lower Galilee; the ancient port city of Akko just north

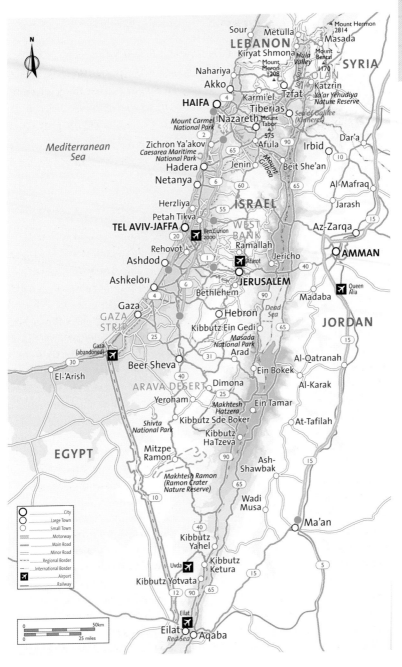

N

Mediterranean
Sea

Sour
Métulla
Mount Hermon
2814
Masada
LEBANON
Kiryat Shmona
Mount
Bental
170
SYRIA
Nahariya
Mount
Meron
1208
Hula
Valley
GOLAN
Akko
Karmi'el
Katzrin
Ya'ar Yehudiya
Nature Reserve
HAIFA
4
Tzfat
Tiberias
Sea of Galilee
(Kinneret)
Mount Carmel
National Park
Nazareth
Mount
Tabor
575
Dar'a
Zichron Ya'akov
Caesarea Maritime
National Park
2
Afula
90
Irbid
Hadera
65
Jenin
Mount Gilboa
Beit She'an
10
Netanya
6
60
65
Al-Mafraq
Herzliya
55
ISRAEL
Jarash
Petah Tikva
WEST
BANK
Az-Zarqa
15
TEL AVIV-JAFFA
Ben Gurion
2000
20
Ramallah
AMMAN
Rehovot
1
Atarot
Jericho
Ashdod
JERUSALEM
40
Queen
Alia
Ashkelon
6
Bethlehem
90
Madaba
Gaza
Hebron
Dead
Sea
JORDAN
GAZA
STRIP
25
Kibbutz Ein Gedi
65
Gaza
(abandoned)
Masada
National Park
Arad
Al-Qatranah
30
Beer Sheva
31
El-'Arish
40
Ein Bokek
Al-Karak
ARAVA DESERT
Dimona
25
Yeroham
Makhtesh
Hatzera
Ein Tamar
Shivta
National Park
Kibbutz Sde Boker
At-Tafilah
EGYPT
Kibbutz
HaTzeva
15
Mitzpe
Ramon
90
Ash-
Shawbak
Makhtesh Ramon
(Ramon Crater
Nature Reserve)
65
Wadi
Musa
10
Ma'an
40
Kibbutz
Yahel
5
Uvda
Kibbutz
Ketura
15
Kibbutz Yotvata
12
90
65
Eilat
Eilat
Red Sea
Aqaba

○ ....City
○ ....Large Town
○ ....Small Town
▨▨▨ ....Motorway
─── ....Main Road
─── ....Minor Road
─ · ─ ....Regional Border
─ · · ─ ....International Border
✈ ....Airport
─── ....Railway

0 ——————— 50km
0 ——————— 25 miles

of Haifa, Beer Sheva which acts as the gateway to the Negev Desert; and Eilat, the Red Sea's party city.

Political geography

The political divisions of this part of the Middle East are hugely complex and ever-changing. Following the Six-Day War in 1967, Israel captured the Syrian lands of the Golan Heights, a 1,790sq km (690sq mile) region it still controls, although classified by the UN as occupied. Because of the political tensions between Syria and Israel, a UN demilitarised zone separates the two countries. On the southern Mediterranean coast bordering Egypt is the Palestinian Territory of the Gaza Strip, and to the east of the Jordanian border is the Palestinian Territory of the West Bank. Since the Six-Day War, when Israel captured Jordanian-ruled East Jerusalem and parts of the West Bank, it has remained in control of these regions (although this is also seen as illegal by the UN and much of the international community) and there remain Israeli settlements within the West Bank.

Climate

Located in a subtropical, Mediterranean region, Israel has two distinct seasons, with predominantly long, hot, dry summers and mild, rainy winters. July and August are the hottest months, which along the central and northern plains and Mediterranean coast can be very humid. This region receives approximately 400mm (15in) of rain annually, the vast majority falling between December and February. Jerusalem and the mountainous regions of the east are considerably less humid in summer, and in winter can get as cold as 6°C (43°F), with snow not unheard of. The southern desert portion of the country has a much drier, hotter climate with temperatures easily reaching 40°C (104°F) in summer and very little rainfall.

Natural environment

Owing to its location on the climatic and geographical crossroads where the northern steppes of Europe meet the Syrian–African Rift Valley, Israel has wonderfully varied flora and fauna. An impressive list includes 2,380 species of flora, from alpine flowers in the north to desert papyrus reeds and the gnarled, ancient olive trees that stud the landscape, as well as more than 110 species of mammal – a striking number when one bears in mind that the whole of Europe boasts just 140 species. The country is also a crucial stopover on the great bird migrations as they make their way north and south twice a year.

Israelis are proud and passionate about the natural environment, to which the country's 66 national parks and 190 nature reserves, under the control of the Israel Nature and National Parks Authority, are a testament. They can be found throughout the country: from the forested hills and rolling valleys of the

Galilee to the wild plains and gushing streams of the Golan and the stark beauty of the craggy deserts and their fertile oases, there are few landscapes not represented in this small country.

Spectacular scenery at the Dead Sea

Wildlife

Israel's unique geographical location between the temperate climate of Europe and the arid desert climate of the south has resulted in a huge number of species of flora and fauna being found throughout the land. Historically, this region was once home to species such as the Syrian brown bear, the cheetah and the Nile crocodile, and conservation efforts are in place to reintroduce more mild-mannered biblical animals back into the landscape.

Mammals

Israel's hugely varied lands support a host of mammals (and indeed all sorts of species of flora and fauna) in its differing climates and ecological regions. Around 116 species of mammal call Israel home, including the striped hyena, jackal, wolf, ibex, wild boar, caracal, hyrax, fallow deer, otter and Asiatic wild ass. There is even a small group of leopards living in the desert hills near the Dead Sea. While species such as the wolf are extremely elusive and many species are nocturnal, mammals such as the jackal, hyrax and ibex are commonly spotted.

Birds

Around 510 species of bird have been spotted in Israel, many passing through on the great migrations north and south. The Hula Valley Nature Reserve and Beit She'an Valley in the Galilee, along with centres in the Arava Desert near Eilat, are world-renowned birdwatching locations as the feathered fliers make crucial pit-stops on the long migratory routes in summer and winter. In the north, the Egyptian vulture and Bonelli's eagles can often be seen soaring through the skies.

Reptiles and marine life

Around 100 species of reptile and 7 species of amphibian (5 of which are endangered) live in Israel. Scorpions live in the desert and snakes can be found in varying habitats around the country.

With four seas, Israel has a rich marine biodiversity (although the Dead Sea's extreme salinity means nothing can in fact live in its waters). Since biblical times, the Sea of Galilee has been an important freshwater fishing site, while Israel's Mediterranean coast is an important nesting site for the highly endangered green sea turtle as well as the large loggerhead turtle. The coral reefs of the Red Sea are home to countless species of tropical fish as well as dolphins and even the occasional whale shark.

Conservation

Huge conservation efforts are in place to reintroduce back into the landscape animals that were hunted to extinction over 100 years ago. The Israel Nature and Parks Authority (*www.parks.org.il*) and the Jerusalem Biblical Zoo (*see p49*) and Ramat Gan Safari Park (*see p157*) are collaborating on conservation projects that have already seen species such as the onager (a wild ass), oryx, roe deer and Persian fallow deer reintroduced into the wild. Wildlife breeding facilities known as Hai Bar have been created in the Arava Desert and on Mount Carmel in an attempt to revive the dwindling numbers of some species or to re-establish those that have not been seen roaming wild for decades. Visitors can experience these animals in their natural habitats, getting the chance to see species such as the wild goat, Ethiopian ostrich and gazelles.

Conservation projects are also under way to help the endangered green sea turtles along the Mediterranean coast, as well as the huge griffon and Egyptian vultures and Bonelli's eagles, which inhabit the skies above the Galilee and Golan Heights.

Leopards can be found in the desert near the Dead Sea

History

Old Testament history

c. 17th century BC Abraham, Isaac and Jacob settle in the land of Canaan. Famine forces the Israelites to relocate to Egypt where they spend 400 years in slavery.

13th–12th century BC Led by Moses, the Israelites escape and spend the following 40 years wandering the desert before settling again in Canaan.

c. 1000 BC King David conquers Jerusalem and names it his capital.

c. 960 BC King Solomon commissions the building of the First Temple in Jerusalem.

8th–6th centuries BC Solomon dies; two kingdoms emerge; Israel and Judah. In 721 BC, the Assyrians conquer Israel and in 586 BC, the Kingdom of Judah falls to the Babylonians, who destroy Jerusalem.

Persian and Hellenistic periods

538 BC Following the Persian conquest of Babylon, the tribe of Judah is granted permission to return to Jerusalem.

515 BC The Second Temple is constructed in Jerusalem.

332 BC Persian rule ends with Alexander the Great's conquest, and the Hellenistic period follows.

166 BC Following years of suppression, the Jews successfully revolt and Jewish religion and culture prevail.

Roman period

63 BC Jerusalem is conquered by the Roman general Pompey.

37 BC Herod the Great is appointed king of Judaea and the great port city of Caesarea is constructed, as well as the palatial clifftop fortress of Masada.

c. AD 8 Jesus of Nazareth is born in Bethlehem.

c. AD 26 Jesus is baptised by John the Baptist and begins his ministry.

c. AD **30**   Jesus is crucified.

AD **70**   Jewish revolts lead to the Romans destroying the Second Temple.

AD **123**   The failed Jewish Bar Kochba revolt results in thousands of Jews being exiled from Roman Palestine. Jerusalem is destroyed and the city of Aelia Capitolina built.

Byzantine and Arab periods

AD **313**   Constantine founds the Byzantine Empire and legalises Christianity. Pilgrims flock to the Holy Land.

AD **632**   The Prophet Muhammad dies and in AD 636 the Arab Islamic Empire conquers Jerusalem.

AD **638**   A shrine is built on the site of the destroyed Second Temple from where Muslim tradition states Muhammad ascended to heaven.

11th century   Jews and Christians are prevented from entering Jerusalem, giving rise to Pope Urban II to call for a crusade to free the city.

The Crusades

1099–1291   Waves of Crusades arrive from Western Europe during which time Jerusalem and the rest of the country are captured and the Muslim and Jewish residents slaughtered. A network of castles appear but eventually the Crusaders are defeated by the Mamluks.

Mamluks and Ottomans

1291–1917   The Mamluk and Ottoman periods see the country enter a dark phase and it suffers economic and population decline. From 1517 until World War I, the Ottoman Turks govern Palestine, and the Jewish population slowly increases.

Zionism

Late 19th–early 20th century   The movement of Jews to create a Jewish homeland (Zionism) begins, spurred on by growing anti-Semitism in Europe and Russia. Tel Aviv is founded, Hebrew revived and the first kibbutz created.

World Wars I and II

1917   The Balfour Declaration states British support for the establishment of a Jewish homeland in Palestine.

| 1920 | The League of Nations gives Britain a 'mandate' to rule Palestine until it believes the local people can govern themselves. Judaism flourishes and Hebrew is recognised as the official language alongside Arabic and English. |

| 1921–30 | Arab unrest at loss of lands and two waves of large-scale Jewish immigration culminates in riots. |

| 1930s | Mass Jewish immigration from Europe after Hitler rises to power. As a result, the British, in 1939, impose a limit on the number of Jewish immigrants allowed into the country. |

| 1939–45 | World War II. The Holocaust in Europe sees the genocide of six million Jews and mass immigration to Palestine. |

A declaration of independence

| 1945–8 | Frictions increase between Jews and Arabs and both revolt against the British. |

| 14 May 1948 | On the same day the British Mandate comes to an end, Israel declares independence, sparking the Arab–Israeli War in which Palestinians are joined by Egypt, Syria, Jordan, Lebanon and Iraq. Israel now controlled 78 per cent of Palestine; Jordan and Egypt took over the remainder. |

A contested land

| 1956 | In the Suez–Sinai War, Israel joins the British and French in the fight against Egyptian nationalisation of the Suez Canal. |

| 1964 | The Palestine Liberation Organization (PLO) is formed. |

| 1967 | The Six-Day War occurs when Israel goes to war with Arab nations. Israel captures East Jerusalem, the West Bank, Gaza, the Sinai Peninsula and the Golan Heights. Attacks on Israel begin. |

| 1969 | Yasser Arafat is elected chairman of the PLO. Israel and Egypt battle in the War of Attrition. |

| 6 October 1973 | Egypt and Syria attack Israel on Yom Kippur but the Israelis emerge |

victorious despite huge loss of life.

1979 Israel and Egypt sign a peace treaty and Sinai is returned to the Egyptians.

1982 In response to attacks by the PLO from Lebanon, Israel attacks and the First Lebanon War ensues. Israel takes southern Lebanon, returning it in 1985.

December 1987 The First Intifada erupts when Palestinians in the West Bank and Gaza launch an uprising against Israeli occupation.

1991 Iraq launches 39 Scud missiles at Israel during the Gulf War.

1995 Israel and the newly formed Palestinian National Authority (PNA) sign the Oslo Accords granting the PNA administrative authority over Gaza and the West Bank. Israeli prime minister, Yitzhak Rabin, is assassinated by a Jewish extremist.

September 2000 Prime Minister Ariel Sharon's visit to the Temple Mount sparks the Second Intifada.

2001–4 Israel constructs a wall around the West Bank.

2005 Israel withdraws all Jewish settlers from the Gaza Strip.

2006 Militant group Hamas kidnaps three Israeli soldiers from the Lebanon and Gaza borders, sparking the Second Lebanon War. A ceasefire is signed in August and the UN steps in to govern southern Lebanon. Hamas wins elections in Gaza, and Israel imposes a blockade (at the time of writing still in place).

December 2008 Following months of rocket attacks, Israel launches an air and ground offensive on Gaza; a ceasefire is achieved in January 2009.

February 2009 Benjamin Netanyahu of the Likud Party is elected prime minister.

May 2009 Tel Aviv celebrates its 100th anniversary.

2010 Israel joins the OECD (Organisation for Economic Co-operation and Development).

The people and religions of Israel

Known to many around the world as the Holy Land, Israel has long been the centre of Judaism and Christianity, and plays a hugely sacred role in Islam. Multiple faiths and denominations revere this land. The Holy Land is awash with important sacred sites. At its heart, Jerusalem has been the centre of battles, miracles, conquests and revolts for centuries; from the Roman Catholics to the Eastern Orthodox, from the Jewish Orthodox to the Druze, and from the Christian Arabs to the Muslims. Of Israel's approximately seven million inhabitants, 76.4 per cent are Jewish, 16 per cent Muslim,2 per cent Christian, 1.6 per cent Druze and a further 4 per cent unclassified.

The white stone buildings of Jerusalem, with the golden Dome of the Rock in their midst, forge an impressive and evocative image. For the Old City stands today as it has through thousands of years. For Jews, the last remnants of the great Temple – the Western Wall – form their most sacred site, long known as the Wailing Wall for the cries of sorrow at the destruction of the Temple. Built on top of the remains of the Temple is the golden Dome of the Rock, revered as the third-holiest site in Islam, the point from where Muhammad ascended to heaven. And within Christianity, the Church of the Holy Sepulchre is regarded as the holiest site of all, standing as it does on the place where tradition states Jesus' crucifixion, burial and resurrection occurred.

Haifa, Israel's third-largest city, set between the shores of the Mediterranean Sea and Mount Carmel, is home to the Shrine of Bahá'u'lláh and the Persian Gardens, one of the two holiest sites within the **Bahá'í** faith and an ornate centrepiece to the city (the other is located just outside Akko). The Bahá'í faith developed in Persia from a branch of Islam and today has over five million adherents around the world.

On Mount Carmel just north of Haifa, and in the wild and barren Golan Heights, live **Druze** communities, known for their wonderful hospitality and traditional dress. Making their living from agriculture, the Druze are highly respected within Israeli society for their peaceful way of life and loyalty to the state. The religion descended from a branch of Islam in the 11th century and is known for its secrecy.

Nazareth, known by **Christians** as the site where Mary received news of the Immaculate Conception, is today home to the country's largest population of Christian Arabs; the grand Church of the Annunciation stands as the central focus of the Old City – an important pilgrimage site for Christians visiting the Holy Land. Following in Jesus' footsteps are the biblical sites around the Sea of Galilee where he performed many of his miracles.

Also on the Sea of Galilee is Tiberias, one of the holy cities of the Jews, with the mystical city of Tzfat not far away in the Upper Galilee region. Renowned as the ancient home of Kabbalah and Jewish learning, here, Hassidic Orthodox Jews wander the streets absorbed in their biblical studies, and an air of tranquillity emanates.

Muslim religious sites centre around Jerusalem, although the once crucial port city of Akko, Tel Aviv's Old City of Jaffa, and towns and villages along the Mediterranean strip are home to large populations of Muslim Arabs. In addition are high numbers of Bedouin, who inhabit the northern stretches of the desert, long having been forced to abandon their traditional nomadic way of life.

Yemenite women preparing street food in Tel Aviv

Politics

The State of Israel declared independence on 14 May 1948 and today it stands as a parliamentary democracy. Though it has a secular government, religion is tightly interwoven in its policies and in the ruling of the country, while the Israeli–Palestinian situation is a constant and seemingly never-ending political crisis.

The government

The running of the country is divided into three authorities: the Knesset, which represents the legislative authority, the government, which is the executive authority, and the judiciary. The Knesset is a 120-member parliament and members, representing a wide range of political parties, are elected every four years. Israel also has a president, elected by the Knesset, but the role is purely ceremonial. Israel's most recent election, in 2009, saw Benjamin Netanyahu at the head of the right-wing Likud party win. It is his second non-consecutive prime-ministerial term.

The economy

In the 63 short years since declaring independence, Israel has managed to create a strong economy with sound infrastructure and a high standard of living. That said, it struggles to cope with factors such as high military and security expenditures, as well as huge influxes of immigrants. Today, its major industries are the production of metal products, electronic and biomedical equipment, processed foods, chemicals, transport equipment, software development and agricultural exports, and it is the world's leading exporter of cut diamonds. In 2010, Israel's GDP reached an estimated $217.1 billion, with a per-capita figure of $29,500, putting it on a

THE IDF

The Israel Defense Forces (IDF) are close to the hearts, emotions and lives of the Israeli people, since both men and women are conscripted to serve at the age of 18. Men serve 3 years and women 21 months, with men serving as reservists for around 1 month per year until the age of 51. Because of Israel's tumultuous political state, military service is active and young Israelis may find themselves in real wars, battles or border skirmishes; many have lost their lives throughout Israel's recent history. Every year in April or May, War Memorial Day is commemorated in a sombre and heartfelt day of remembrance.

par with many major European countries.

The Israeli–Palestinian conflict

The Israeli–Palestinian conflict refers to the long-standing and ongoing hostilities between the State of Israel and the Palestinian people. After World War I, many Jews emigrated to Palestine, leading to a contest with the Palestinians over land that continued to be a barrier to peace after Israel's establishment. Today, the remaining key issues centre around border disputes, the control of Jerusalem, Israeli settlements in parts of the West Bank, and Palestinian freedom of movement. The Gaza Strip, under the control of Hamas, is under Israeli blockade as a result of continuous rocket fire on bordering Israeli towns.

The conflict has been a bloody and violent one, with high numbers of Palestinian deaths and repeated terrorist attacks within Israel, giving rise to the construction of a wall around parts of the West Bank. Extremely tight security within Israel means attacks are far less common these days, however, and visitors should not be any more concerned about terrorism here than they would be in their own country.

Israeli President Shimon Peres

Culture

An ancient heritage, waves of immigration from across the world, a mixture of religions, culinary styles, languages and arts have all combined to give Israel one of the most interesting, varied and eclectic cultures in the world. Yet despite this melting pot and its unique demographic make-up, Israel's overall culture is one that is proud and has a strong sense of identity and unity.

Although Israel was founded as the Jewish state, countless other faiths, nationalities and religions make up the complex demographics, and today Muslim and Christian Arabs, Eastern and Roman Orthodox, Druze, Bedouin, and Palestinians – who do not identify themselves as Israelis at all – live alongside Jews of various descent. In addition, there have been large numbers of Russian immigrants as well as Thai, Philippine and Chinese migrant workers. All of this means that Israel has an extremely fast growth rate, having increased from a population of 650,000 to more than 7,000,000 in 60 years.

It is therefore not surprising that national identity is a very complex sentiment, particularly because for Jewish residents, faith and citizenship are one and the same thing. However, even within Judaism there are differing standpoints, for there is a large number of secular Jews in Israel, for whom Judaism is more of a cultural and ethnic identity than a religious one. Despite – or perhaps precisely because of – the complexities of this melting pot, each religious group has freedom to govern its own holy sites and, for the most part, the people living in this land coexist in relative harmony.

While much of the cultural life of Israel thus revolves around religion and its expression in the form of festivals, events, architecture and other arts, there is more to the vibrant culture of

PLACE NAMES

Both Hebrew and Arabic are the official languages of Israel, and both have their own alphabets. Spellings of place names in the Roman alphabet can therefore often vary hugely. In addition to this, places and sites can often be referred to by a different name according to who is speaking. English is widely spoken in Israel, all road signs are displayed in Hebrew, Arabic and English, and many religious sites are known only by their English names. Because of these issues, most place names within this guide are given in English.

this country than just religion, and visitors looking for a full and rich cultural experience in Israel won't be disappointed.

Architecture

Many of Israel's cities are ancient, their roots dating back centuries. Architectural styles reflect the different rulers, immigrants and religions that have made their mark on the country. Tel Aviv's Bauhaus architecture earned it UNESCO World Heritage status, while Jerusalem, Tzfat, Jaffa, Nazareth and Akko's Old Cities have buildings

that are centuries old. Over time, colonies and neighbourhoods appeared in cities such as Jerusalem, Tel Aviv and Haifa, each emanating the architectural styles of the new occupants' native countries or religious beliefs.

Arts

Art, music, theatre, dance and cinema have a proud place within Israeli culture. World-class art galleries such as Tel Aviv's Museum of Art display works from top Israeli artists, while villages such as Ein Hod and Rosh Pina are dedicated to the development of art.

Culture

A jet fighter on display at the Beer Sheva Air Force Museum

The Israeli Philharmonic Orchestra plays to sell-out performances at its home in Tel Aviv and is host to guest conductors from around the world, while several other cities also have successful and well-respected orchestras. Modern music is also big business within Israel, and cities such as Tel Aviv and Haifa come alive at weekends, with huge trance parties, nightclubs and concerts. Increasingly, more foreign artists are now including Israel in their world tours, and these attract thousands of excited Israelis.

A street performer in Tel Aviv

Tel Aviv's HaBima Theatre hosts Hebrew and English performances from top theatrical troupes, while ballet and dance are on the rise. Cinema is also at the forefront of Israeli culture, with topics mostly focusing on historical and political events. The Tel Aviv and Jerusalem cinematheques and Spielberg Film Archive are the centres for Jewish and Israeli cinematography.

Literature

Eliezer Ben Yehuda (1858–1922) is credited with reviving the Hebrew language and establishing it as the modern language spoken in Israel today. With the advent of this modernised form came a wave of new literature, with topics often focused on Zionism, ideology and religion. Later, the Holocaust, wars and the political situation formed core topics. In addition to the large volume of Hebrew literature, many books written by Jews and Israelis in other languages are extant, including works in Arabic, English, French and Russian.

Museums

The country is home to some outstanding museums. From the sobering Yad Vashem Holocaust Memorial Museum to the Israel Museum, with displays ranking among the most important in the world, to Tel Aviv's galleries and Haifa's naval and maritime museums, every aspect of culture and history is documented.

A gunboat at the Israeli National Maritime Museum

CULTURAL ETIQUETTE

Navigating cultural etiquette in Israel can be a rather intimidating prospect for visitors, given the complexities of this country in which most of the customs and protocols revolve around religious taboos. On the one hand, Israel is a casual, laid-back country where people are loud, rough-around-the-edges and don't mince their words yet wear their hearts on their sleeves and are welcoming to visitors. But on the other hand, devout religious observance in many areas means that a sensitive, respectful approach is the best, and indeed only, way to ensure that you don't deeply offend or upset the local people among whom you are a guest. Keeping the following points in mind should help prevent you from making any faux pas:

Dress: In any religious building or neighbourhood, ensure you dress modestly. This usually means the covering of shoulders and legs down to the knee for women. Carrying a shawl or scarf at all times is advisable, especially in cities such as Jerusalem, but in Orthodox Jewish neighbourhoods, long skirts (not trousers) and long-sleeved blouses are necessary.

Greetings: *Shalom* is the usual greeting, although on Shabbat, *Shabbat Shalom* is used instead. Handshaking is common, but women should always wait for a man's hand to be extended first, as observant male Jews are not permitted to touch women.

Taboos: Within the Muslim culture it is offensive to show the sole of your foot, and the left hand is also considered unclean, so shake hands or eat only with your right hand. Women must not touch observant Jewish men, so be sensitive on public transport or in crowded areas and try not to get too close. Avoid any public displays of affection in religious sites. This applies to Jewish and Muslim religious sites as well as ultra-Orthodox neighbourhoods, and applies to both heterosexual and (considerably more so) to homosexual couples. Fasting during both the Muslim holiday of Ramadan and the Jewish holiday of Yom Kippur is strictly followed and you should abstain from drinking alcohol or eating (and in the case of Muslim areas during Ramadan, smoking) in public areas during these times.

Festivals and events

Israelis are a passionate people who, despite hardships over the years, wear their hearts on their sleeves. The vast majority of festivals in the country centre around Jewish religious days, most of which are national holidays. Yet alongside these, music, the arts, Gay Pride, Independence Day or Holocaust Memorial Day are all celebrated with heartfelt excitement or sorrow.

Holidays pertain to the Jewish calendar and so change yearly on the Gregorian calendar. Jewish holidays begin an hour before sunset and finish one hour after sunset the following day. For details, visit *www.thinkisrael.com*

March

Purim (8 Mar 2012, 24 Feb 2013) Celebrated in honour of Queen Esther. Israelis don fancy dress and enjoy a fun-filled evening of festivities and parties.

April

Pesach (Passover) (7–14 Apr 2012, 25 Mar–2 Apr 2013) Celebrates the Exodus when Moses freed the slaves from Egypt and is today remembered with a special dinner known as the *Seder*, at which symbolic foods are eaten and readings given. The 40 days and nights of the Exodus are commemorated by abstaining from eating unleavened bread.
Holocaust Memorial Day (19 Apr 2012, 8 Apr 2013) A sombre and emotional day of remembrance for the

six million Jews who lost their lives in one of the world's worst genocides.
War Memorial Day (25 Apr 2012) Commemorates the fallen soldiers of Israel's wars and is a painful and sad day in the country.
Independence Day (26 Apr 2012, 16 Apr 2013) At the close of War Memorial Day, the country erupts into vibrant festivities in celebration of its declaration of independence. Street parties are held throughout the country.
Easter Parade Thousands of Christians carrying large wooden crosses follow in Jesus' last footsteps along the Via Dolorosa in Jerusalem's Old City (*see pp52–3*).

May

Lag Ba'Omer (10 May 2012) The last day of the mourning period known as Omer is celebrated on this day. Tradition has it that a plague afflicted Rabbi Akiva's students and ended upon this day. It is celebrated at Mount Meron by Orthodox familes.

Shavuot (Pentacost) (27 May 2012, 15 May 2013) Also known as the Harvest Festival, it was in ancient times celebrated by bringing food offerings to the Temple of Jerusalem. It also commemorates the day the Torah was given to the Jewish people at Mount Sinai.

Israel Festival (May–June) Held in concert halls around Jerusalem, the festival celebrates theatre, dance and classical music performances.

June

Gay Pride (8 June 2012) Tel Aviv shows off its liberal, secular colours in a fun, happy parade through the city's streets.

July

Jerusalem Film Festival A wide variety of genres and styles of film and documentaries are showcased in cinemas around the city.

August

Clarinet and Klezmer in the Galilee (Aug 2012) A week-long festival of

The Tamar Festival is held during Sukkot

evening performances by top Israeli classical, jazz and Klezmer performers. Held in the Jewish holy city of Tzfat.

September

Rosh HaShana (Jewish New Year) (17–18 Sept 2012, 5–6 Sept 2013) Resolutions are made for the upcoming year at this time of happiness and reflection. Israelis also enjoy Sylvester (New Year on the Gregorian calendar).

October

Yom Kippur (Day of Atonement) (26 Sept 2012, 14 Sept 2013) Judaism's holiest day is a time of fasting, repentance and prayer. The country closes down for 25 hours and it is a special experience as the streets empty of cars, television stations shut down and children ride bicycles along deserted motorways.

Sukkot (Feast of Tabernacles) (1 Oct 2012, 19 Sept 2013) Along with Pesach (Passover), Sukkot celebrates the Exodus when Moses freed the slaves from Egypt.

Acco (Akko) Festival of Alternative Israeli Theatre (Oct 2012) National theatre groups perform mainly Hebrew plays and performances. *www.accofestival.co.il*

December

Hannukah (15–19 Dec 2012, 28 Nov– 5 Dec 2013) Celebrates the victory of the Macabbees in the battle for Jerusalem. Using a special candelabra, one candle is lit every day for the eight days of the festival.

Highlights

N

Mount Hermon 2814

LEBANON

Masada

Kiryat Shmona

Hula Valley

Mount Bental 1170

GOLAN

SYRIA

Nahariya

Mount Meron 1208

Akko

HAIFA ❽

Karmi'el

Tzfat ❹

Katzrin

Tiberias

Sea of Galilee (Kinneret) ❺

Nazareth

Mount Tabor 575

Mount Carmel National Park

Zichron Ya'akov

Afula

Irbid

Mediterranean Sea

Hadera ❻

Jenin

Beit She'an

Netanya

Herzliya

ISRAEL

Petah Tikva

TEL AVIV-JAFFA ❸

Ben Gurion 2000

WEST BANK

Rehovot

Ramallah

Jericho

AMMAN

Ashdod

Atarot

Ashkelon

❶ **JERUSALEM**

Bethlehem

Gaza

GAZA STRIP

Hebron

Dead Sea ❷

Kibbutz Ein Gedi

JORDAN

Gaza (abandoned)

Arad

El 'Arish

Beer Sheva

Ein Bokek

ARAVA DESERT Dimona

Yeroham

Ein Tamar

Kibbutz Sde Boker

Kibbutz HaTzeva

EGYPT

Mitzpe Ramon ❿

Makhtesh Ramon (Ramon Crater Nature Reserve)

Kibbutz Yahel

Uvda

Kibbutz Ketura

Kibbutz Yotvata

Eilat

Eilat ❼

Red Sea Aqaba

❶ Absorbing the intrigue of Jerusalem's Old City, one of the most historically profound and religiously significant places in the world, and the site where Judaism, Christianity and Islam meet (*see p32*).

❷ Floating in the Dead Sea, the world's lowest point, famed for its therapeutic, salty waters and extreme buoyancy (*see p123*).

❸ Partying in Tel Aviv, where throngs of young Israelis fill the city's trendiest cafés, bars and nightclubs (*see p54*).

❹ Soaking up the atmosphere in Tzfat Old City, where the quiet, cobbled streets of Judaism's 'mystical city' emanate biblical learning and devout study (*see p100*).

❺ Enjoying the beauty and history of the Sea of Galilee and following in Jesus' footsteps in the green valleys and tranquil waters at the sites of his miracles and baptism (*see p95*).

❻ Visiting the Caesarea Maritime National Park, one of the world's most crucial ancient port cities and once home to the Roman governor Pontius Pilate, Herod the Great and the Crusaders (*see p84*).

❼ Snorkelling in the Red Sea, Israel's most southern point and home to pretty coral reefs, tropical fish, year-round warm waters and glitzy hotels (*see p130*).

❽ Marvelling at the grandeur of the Bahá'í Shrine and Persian Gardens of Haifa, the headquarters of the Bahá'í faith and the ornate centrepiece of this relaxed, laid-back city (*see p70*).

❾ Exploring Akko's Old City, with its strong city walls, abundance of historical buildings, cobbled alleys, bustling market and quaint fishing port (*see p78*).

❿ Hiking in the Makhtesh Ramon, the heart of the great southern deserts and a geological marvel (*see p122*).

Floating in the Dead Sea near Ein Gedi

Suggested itineraries

Long weekend

The jewel in Israel's crown is undoubtedly Jerusalem, and so the best part of a long weekend should be spent exploring this city. Begin in the Old City and allow for at least a day of wandering the cobbled lanes, getting lost amid the bustling bazaars and being awestruck by the religious buildings. On day two, move outside the city walls to the Mount of Olives where a morning of brisk walking or easy driving will reveal sites of interest. Spend the afternoon in the sobering Yad Vashem Holocaust Memorial Museum, where the stories of the millions of Jews that perished are told in grim truth. On day three, take a trip, either by public bus or car, down to the Dead Sea, the saltiest body of water on earth and also the lowest land point, at 400m (1,312ft) below sea level. Take a dip in the buoyant water, embark on a hike in the Ein Gedi Nature Reserve or visit the impressive hilltop ruins of Masada. For the last day, get to know the neighbourhoods of the new city of Jerusalem, such as the ultra-Orthodox Mea Shearim, the pretty German Colony or the rustic Mahane Yehuda with the traditional covered market at its centre.

One week

A week in Israel is best divided between Jerusalem, the Dead Sea, Tel Aviv and the Galilee. Follow the itinerary as for a long weekend above, but combine a trip to Yad Vashem and the new city into one day, omitting the Mount of Olives. This leaves four more days in which to see more of Israel's landscape. Allow for a day in Tel Aviv-Jaffa, where you can soak up the atmosphere from a cool café, visit the Tel Aviv Museum of Art and, if time allows, pop along the coast to Jaffa Old City. Save some energy for a couple of late evening drinks in a trendy bar.

From Tel Aviv, head north to Akko, the great port city that once defeated

The impressive ruins at Masada

Charming old house in Jaffa

Two weeks

Once again, begin your trip in Jerusalem and allow three days to fully explore the Old City, Mount of Olives, new city, Yad Vashem and the Israel Museum. On day four, head down to the Dead Sea where you can spend two days hiking in Ein Gedi Nature Reserve, visiting Masada and lounging in one of the spas. From there, continue south to Mitzpe Ramon and allow for two days of desert activities, becoming one with nature at an eco lodge and hiking in the Makhtesh Ramon (Ramon Crater Nature Reserve).

For week two, head north to Tel Aviv and spend two days relaxing in the party city, eating excellent food, lounging on the wide sandy beaches or visiting ancient Jaffa or the wealth of museums. Head north and visit Caesarea Maritime National Park's incredible ruins before heading to Haifa, Israel's third-largest city. Spend a day walking the steep topography and marvelling at the Bahá'í Gardens and Shrine. From there, it is on to Akko for a day of Crusader history and walking the ramparts, before spending the last two days in the Galilee. Nazareth Old City and the peaceful green shores of the Sea of Galilee with its biblical history can be visited in a leisurely manner, rounding up a busy but fulfilling two-week trip. This itinerary can easily be completed using public transport – either bus or train – except for Caesarea Maritime National Park, which can only be reached by car. The

Napoleon. Amble through the Crusader ruins of this bustling Arab city, peruse the stalls of the souk and enjoy fresh fish caught from the busy fishing port. The next morning head over to the Galilee and spend a morning exploring Nazareth's Old City, with its Christian traditions and churches, Arab souk and old-world charm. From there, head across to the Sea of Galilee and watch the sun set over the lake. All of the above can easily be done by public bus or by car.

train runs from Tel Aviv to Akko via Haifa, and all other destinations mentioned have regular bus services.

Longer

If you are lucky enough to have a substantial amount of time in which to travel in Israel, there is a whole host of incredible experiences that can supplement the two-week itinerary. Using the above itinerary as a framework, you can add side trips to enhance your understanding of the country's complex history, varied geography and fascinating cultures. From Mitzpe Ramon, drop down to Eilat on the Red Sea for some Middle Eastern scuba diving, beach lazing and partying, before heading up through the Arava with its unique eco lodges, Hai Bar Wildlife Reserve and Timna Park. Pass Mitzpe Ramon and stop at Sde Boker for a few hours, the home and final resting place of Israel's first prime minister, David Ben Gurion.

Along the Mediterranean coast, spend an afternoon in between Caesarea and Haifa in the irrepressibly charming Zichron Ya'akov at the base of Mount Carmel. The picturesque town was founded by the grandfather of Zionism, Baron Edmond de Rothschild, and is home to the country's largest and first winery.

In the Galilee, visit the sprawling, impressive Roman ruins at Beit She'an and allow for extra time to walk in Jesus' footsteps around the Sea of Galilee. From there, head into the remote and wild Golan Heights, where horse riding and jeep tours, hiking in the Ya'ar Yehudiya Nature Reserve, enjoying traditional Druze food and hospitality, and ascending the towering Mount Hermon are just some of the highlights.

Drop down into the Upper Galilee through the Hula Valley, famed as one of the crucial stopovers for the vast north–south bird migrations, and then visit the Jewish holy city of Tzfat, where cobbled lanes, traditionally clad

Tzfat, an ethereal place in which to lose oneself

Colourful Druze trinkets on sale at Daliat al-Carmel

Orthodox Jews and an artists' quarter give it the quiet feel of yesteryear.

The above itinerary involves much more off-the-beaten-track destinations, but most of it can be achieved with public transport. The main exceptions are the Golan Heights and desert, where public transport is limited (often one or two buses a day), so having a car is a big advantage.

Jerusalem

Jerusalem is the jewel in the crown of a trip to Israel. It is the centre of three world religions and home to grand religious sites, historical wonders and archaeological treasures. The Old City forms the central focus of interest to visitors, although the new city neighbourhoods are certainly worth exploring.

The haphazard jumble of buildings within the Old City symbolises a tumultuous history in which, for millennia, this place was a decisive battlefield for those fighting in the name of religion, while the new city neighbourhoods, in their architectural styles, culture and ambience, stand as a clear reflection of those who built them.

While Jerusalem is a modern and cosmopolitan city with world-class universities, an efficient transport network and thriving business sector, it is undoubtedly traditional. In this city, religious observance prevails, the majority of restaurants are kosher, Shabbat (the Sabbath, observed from Friday sunset to Saturday sunset) is a time for quiet reflection, and centuries-old buildings are commonplace.

Jerusalem has always marked the final battle for the land and stands as possibly the most sought-after and disputed city in the world. While day-to-day life carries on mostly

uneventfully, and for the most part the different people, religions and cultures coexist in relative (albeit tentative) contentment, this is a city of passionate and devout people who cherish the Holy City.

OLD CITY

Jerusalem's Old City stands as one of the most religiously significant, historically compelling and intriguing places on earth. On the 100ha (247-acre) soils of the Old City, vicious and passionate battles took place, some of the greatest legends of our past stood, and three world religions met. The hotchpotch of buildings within the Old City is broadly divided into four quarters: Christian, Jewish, Muslim and Armenian. Each has its own characteristics and makes for a fascinating experience as visitors move from vibrant market streets to quiet churches to bustling plazas. While each quarter is basically home to the worshippers of a single religion (the

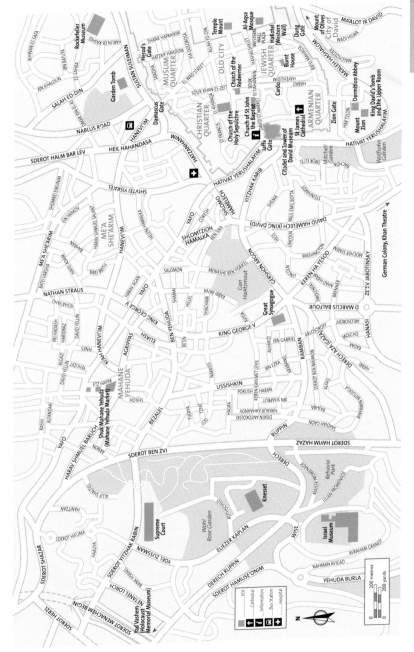

MA'ALOT IR DAVID
Mount of Olives
City of David
WADI HILWA
MA'ALEH HASHALOM
Dung Gate
Dormition Abbey
King David's Tomb and The Upper Room
Zion Gate
Mount Zion
HATIVAT YERUSHALAYIM
Wohl John Garden
MACHPELA
German Colony, Khan Theatre

Temple Mount
Al-Aqsa Mosque
HASHALSHELET
WESTERN WALL
Hakotel (Western Wall)
JEWISH QUARTER
HAYEHUDIM
HABAD
Burnt House
Cardo
St James' Cathedral
ARMENIAN QUARTER
MITCHELL Garden
DROR ELITE

OLD CITY
ALLAH ED-DIN
VIA DOLOROSA
Church of the Redeemer
SOUK EL-DABBAGHA
Church of the Holy Sepulchre
SOUK ST MARKET
DAVID ST MARKET
Citadel and Tower of David Museum
Jaffa Gate
PAUL EMIL BOTTA
STEINHARDT
SHEMA
DAVID HAMELECH (KING DAVID)
HESS
LINCOLN
WASHINGTON
GERSHON AGRON
MOCHEN SHARIM
BRENNER
KEREN HA YESOD
AHAD HA'AM
ABARBANEL
ZE'EV JABOTINSKY

Herod's Gate
SHAAR HAPRANIM
HATZRIF HAADOM
SA'DIA
EL-WAD STREET
MUSLIM QUARTER
SOUK KHAN ES-ZEIT
CHRISTIAN QUARTER
ST FRANCIS
ELKHANDA
Church of St John the Baptist

SHAAR HAPRANIM
SULTAN SULEIMAN
Damascus Gate
HANEVI'IM
HATZVANIM
WINWINZAHAV
HATIVAT YERUSHALAYIM
YITZHAK KARIB
HAMELECH SHLOMO
YAFO
CORESH
SHLOMTZION HAMALKA
BEN SIRA
Gan HaAtzmaut
MENASHE BEN YISRAEL
Great Synagogue
RABBI AKIVA
HILLEL
SHAMAI
BEN YEHUDA
BETZ
D MARCUS BALFOUR
ARLOSOROFF
HANASI
BALFOUR
RAMBAN
IBN GABIROL
IBN EZRA
SDEROT BEN MAIMON
ALFASI
DERECH AZA (GAZA)
HANASI
MOLCHO
RADAK
HA'ARI

Rockefeller Museum
HA'RUN ER-RASHID
IKHWAN ES-SAFA
IBN BATUTA
ZZ ZAHRA
IBN KHALDUN
Garden Tomb
SALAH ED-DIN
OMAR IBN EL KHATAB
NABLUS ROAD
HANEVI'IM
HEIL HAHANDASA
SDEROT HAIM BAR LEV
SHIVTEI YISRA'EL
SHOMREI EMUNIM
ME'A SHE'ARIM
EIN YA'AKOV
HARAV SHMUEL SALANT
HELEN HAMALKA
BA'AL HATUR
BA'EL SHEM
HARAV AGAN
YAFO
HARAV YEHUDA
KING GEORGE V
AGRIPPAS
ELIASHIV
KIKAR HANEVI'IM

NATHAN STRAUS
YESHAYAHU
BATEI VARSHA
PRI HADASH
HARDBAZ
DAVID YELLIN
PINES
ALGAZI
YEHUDIT
DAVID YELLIN
RASHI
ALFANDARI
YAFO
HARAV SHMUEL BARUCH
NONA
AMRAM
BEZALEL
ETZ HAYIM
MAHANE YEHUDA
Shuk Mahane Yehuda (Mahane Yehuda Market)
HOTZVIM
KING GEORGE V
BE'ER
MARKES
USSISHKIN
PORUSH HARAN
KEREN HARAN
IBN SHAPRUT
HAKALIR KAHANOV
DISKIN ANTOKOLSKI
TVERIA
GAD
IZAT
HAGRA
BASHBA
SA'ADIA GAON
BINYAMIN MITUDELA
SDEROT HAVIM HAZAZ
RUPPIN
DERECH
NAYOT
MASSETE MOSHE
BEIT HAKEREM
JULIAN PROMENADE
Rehavia Park
SDEROT BEN ZVI
Supreme Court
Wohl Rose Garden
Knesset
ELIEZER KAPLAN
WYSE
Israel Museum
RUPPIN
RUTHSCHILD
YOEL ZUSSMAN
SDEROT YITZHAK RABIN
NETANEL LORCH
ALUF SHALTIEL
HANITZAN
SDEROT HA'UMA
HALIYA
BANK ISRAEL
SDEROT SHAZAR
SDEROT HERZL
SDEROT MENACHEM BEGIN
Yad Vashem (Holocaust Memorial Museum)
DERECH RUPPIN
SDEROT HAMUSE'ONIM
AVRAHAM GRANOT
NAHMAN AVIGAD
YEHUDA BURLA

POI
Cathedral
Information
Bus Station
Hospital
N
0   200 metres
0   200 yards

Armenian population being Christian), the maze of historical and religious buildings tumble into each other and it is easy – and highly recommended – to simply get lost amid them all.

Burnt House and Wohl Archaeological Museum

The area upon which today stands the Jewish Quarter was considered the most affluent neighbourhood during the Second Temple period until it was sacked by the Romans in AD 70. The **Burnt House** was but one casualty of this and was excavated and converted into a museum to depict life during the Herodian era. Likewise, the more impressive remains housed within the nearby **Wohl Archaeological Museum** display remains of affluent mansions and their contents.

Burnt House, Tiferet Y'Israel St. Tel: (02) 628 7211. Open: Sun–Thur 9am–5pm, Fri 9am–1pm. Admission charge.
Wohl Archaeological Museum, 1 Hakara'im St. Tel: (02) 628 3448. Open: Sun–Thur 9am–5pm, Fri 9am–1pm. Admission charge.

Cardo

This once formed the heart of Roman Jerusalem, the colonnaded street running for 200m (220yds) through the city. Today, it sits in the midst of the Jewish Quarter and is a gentle melée of Judaica and art shops, cafés and small restaurants. A section has been excavated to show how it once appeared.

Cardo, the heart of Roman Jerusalem

Churches

The Old City's churches represent the diverse Christian denominations that pray within them. The holiest and grandest is the Church of the Holy Sepulchre (*see below*); however, several others are most certainly worth discovering. In Muristan Square, the **Church of St John the Baptist**, reputedly housing its namesake's remains, is the oldest church in the city. It acted as a hospice for injured soldiers during the Crusades, giving rise to the order of the Knights Hospitaller. Also within the square is the Protestant **Lutheran Church of the Redeemer**, which was given to Kaiser Wilhelm II of Germany by the Ottomans in 1898. There is a spectacular panorama from the top of the church tower that is well worth the climb. Hidden down in the quiet Armenian Quarter is the ornately decorated **St James Cathedral**, so named because tradition states that both Jesus' brother and James the Apostle are buried within. A visit during an Armenian Orthodox Mass sees the entire church illuminated by hanging lanterns. Just outside the Old City on Mount Zion is the impressive **Dormition Abbey** with its attractive conical blue roof. It is revered by several Christian denominations as the site upon which Mary supposedly ascended to heaven.

Church of St John the Baptist, Muristan Square. Open: irregular hours.
Free admission.
Lutheran Church of the Redeemer, Muristan Square. Tel: (02) 627 6111. Open: daily 9am–1pm & 1.30–3pm. Free admission, but admission charge for clock tower.
St James Cathedral, Armenian Patriarchate St. Open: daily 8am–5pm. Free admission.
Dormition Abbey, Mount Zion. Tel: (02) 565 5330. Open: Mon–Fri 8.30am–noon & 12.40–6pm, Sat 8.30am–noon & 12.40–5.30pm, Sun 10.30–11.45am & 12.40–5.30pm. Free admission.

Church of the Holy Sepulchre

Revered as the most important site in Christianity, the church was built over the sites where the crucifixion, burial and resurrection of Jesus Christ are believed to have taken place. Pilgrims from across the world pour through the doors into the cavernous church, with architectural styles reflecting the different denominations that have for centuries quarrelled over its development. The church holds a wealth of historically intriguing and ecclesiastically significant sites, including the **Unction Stone** that dominates the doorway, revered as the site where Jesus' body was laid out, and **Calvary (Golgotha)**, around which the church was built. It is here that tradition holds that Jesus was crucified and his body removed from the cross. Surrounded by flickering candles and a patient queue of worshippers is the **Rotunda**, worshipped as Jesus' tomb. A maze of ornately decorated corridors and chapels weave into the darkness, adding to the church's intrigue. Even

The Church of the Holy Sepulchre

the most apathetic of visitors will find themselves moved by the passion this place evokes.

Open: 4.30am–7pm. Free admission.

Citadel and Tower of David Museum

The unmistakable citadel has played a major part in almost all of the city's major episodes, each conqueror refortifying it for his own purposes. King Herod and the Romans, the Crusaders, the Mamluks and the Ottomans (during which time the mosque and minaret were built) all commandeered it, and it was on the steps of the citadel that General Allenby declared freedom of religion in 1917. Today, a hugely impressive museum occupies the heart of the citadel, providing a wealth of interactive information on the history of Jerusalem.

Jaffa Gate entrance. Tel: (02) 626 5333. www.towerofdavid.org.il. Open: Sat–Thur 10am–5pm, Fri 10am–2pm. Admission charge.

City gates

Eleven gates once led into the Old City, but today just seven are open, each as much part of its history as the buildings within it. The walls as we see them today were built during the Ottoman period and are a wonderful example of Islamic architecture. The busiest gates are **Jaffa Gate**, which is the main entrance, and the impressive **Damascus Gate**, which is used by residents of East Jerusalem to access the busy souks and Al-Aqsa Mosque. **Zion Gate** (or Bab El-Nabi Daoud) leads out of the Armenian Quarter on to Mount Zion. It was used by the IDF (Israel Defense Forces) in 1967 to enter and capture the Old City and bears bullet scars to this day. Also on the southern wall, the **Dung Gate** (so named because it is believed rubbish was taken out through it) forms the main entrance to the Western Wall and Temple Mount. **Herod's Gate**, which opens on to East Jerusalem, is famed as the point where the Crusaders breached the walls and declared Jerusalem part of the Latin Kingdom. Long closed, the **Golden Gate** sits in the wall encompassing the Temple Mount complex. According to Jewish tradition, it is through this gate that the Messiah will enter Jerusalem.

Tower of David

Praying at the Western Wall

HaKotel (Western Wall)

Millions of Jews from all over the world have come to pray at HaKotel, revered as the holiest site in Judaism. The Western Wall is the last remaining remnant of the Second Temple and has long been referred to as the Wailing Wall for the cries of sorrow that have been shed over its destruction. Today, the Western Wall is the single-most important site in the Jewish faith and an important pilgrimage site and centre of daily prayer where Jews place their prayers. Sitting at the base of the vast Western Wall Plaza, the wall is divided into two prayer sections: men to the left and women to the right. Security checks are conducted at each of the three entrances into the plaza, and modest dress is mandatory; women must cover their shoulders and legs above the knees, and paper yarmulkes (prayer caps) are provided for men wishing to approach the wall.

Beneath the plaza run the Western Wall Tunnels, which have been excavated to unearth further sections of the Second Temple. Guided tours reveal the complex history of this part of the Old City (book in advance).
Open: 24 hours. Free admission. Western Wall Tunnels. Tel: (02) 627 1333. www.thekotel.org. Open: Sun–Thur 7am–last tour booking, Fri 7am–noon. Admission charge.

King David's Tomb and the Upper Room

Located just outside the Old City in the area known as Mount Zion, these two sites can be found one above the other, and are venerated by Jews and Christians. On the ground floor is the ornate tomb of King David. It is one of Judaism's holiest sites and surrounded by yeshivas (religious schools). On the first floor of the building is the site known as the Upper Room which, tradition has it, was the site of the Last Supper and the place where Jesus

King David's Tomb

established the rite of the Eucharist. While there isn't an awful lot to see here, it marks a crucial pilgrimage stop for scores of visitors.

King David's Tomb. Open: Sat–Thur 8am–5pm, Fri 8am–1pm. Free admission.

Upper Room. Open: daily 8am–5pm. Free admission.

Souks

The bustling, energetic souks (bazaars) weave through the cobbled lanes where a maze of shops sell everything from rosary beads to menorahs to spices. Leading down from the busy Jaffa Gate entrance is David Street market, which splits into Souk El-Lahannin, Souk El-Attarin and Souk El-Khawadjat at the bottom. Souvenir, art, craft and

A bustling Jerusalem souk

WALKING THE RAMPARTS

Starting from Jaffa Gate, steps lead up on to the top of the ramparts and make for a wonderful view of the Old City and the beginning of a very pleasant walk. The path leads almost fully around the walls, where a mesh of church spires, clock towers, domed roofs and mosque minarets vie for space within the cramped 100ha (247 acres) of the Old City. The path stops along the Temple Mount wall, where it is possible to descend to the Ophel Promenade outside the walls and continue at ground level to the Dung Gate, where the path once again leads on to the walls.

religious artefact shops are crammed together as tourists haggle their way through the labyrinthine streets. While this market is undoubtedly fun, a more authentic souk experience is to be had in the Muslim Quarter, home to active street markets that form an important part of daily life. Sumptuous bakeries, rustic eateries and jewellery vie for space amid the crowds of locals. Two streets, El-Wad Street and Souk Khan es-Zeit, lead down from Damascus Gate and are a feast of aromatic scents, vibrant colours and noisy hubbub.

Synagogues

Located in the tranquil Jewish Quarter are several synagogues, the mere existence of which is testament to the turbulent life of Jerusalem. The newly renovated **Hurva Synagogue** now takes pride of place on Hurva Square and is easily identified by its clean, white dome. First built by Rabbi Yehuda HaNassi in 1701, it has been the spiritual centre of Askenazi Jews despite several episodes of abandonment or destruction. Today, it once again stands in all its glory. A similar scene played out in the **Rambam Synagogue**, which was named in honour of Rabbi Moshe Ben Nachman (Rambam). He built the synagogue in 1267 amid the rubble of the city following the battle between the Crusaders and the Mamluks. Since Israel's declaration of independence, this synagogue has become the most important site of worship in the Old City. The nearby **Four Sephardi Synagogues** were built within one building, each representing the history and roots of those who pray there, from Spanish Jews to those from Turkey. It is also famed as the final place to be taken when the Jordanians took control of the city in 1948.

Hurva Synagogue. Free admission.
Rambam Synagogue. Free admission.
Four Sephardi Synagogues. Tel: (02) 628 0592. Open: Sun–Thur 9.30am–4pm, Fri 9.30am–12.30pm. Free admission.

Temple Mount

The golden Dome of the Rock is a glittering landmark on the Jerusalem skyline, sitting in the midst of the Temple Mount complex. Against the hustle and bustle of the narrow lanes of the Old City, the Temple Mount is a complete contrast. The spacious, tree-studded complex contains the third-holiest site in Islam – the **Al-Aqsa Mosque** built in the early 8th century. Despite its peaceful atmosphere (except

Dome of the Rock

on Fridays when thousands of Muslims pour in for prayer), the Temple Mount has long been the centre of the turmoil that has existed until this day between Jews and Muslims. For this site is also revered by Jews as the spot upon which the First and Second Temples stood and where the Foundation Stone (upon which the world was built) stands. The Dome of the Rock and Al-Aqsa Mosque are closed to non-Muslims, but the complex itself is a wonderful and serene place to visit, although it is important to realise the extreme sensitivities of this site and pay heed to political changes and religious law.

Tel: (02) 628 3292. Open: Sun–Thur 7.30–10am & 12.30–1.30pm.
Free admission.

The Holy City

Jerusalem stands as the most revered city in the world: different faiths, denominations and peoples have worshipped the sacred ground upon which it stands for centuries. From biblical days, when the Canaanites and Israelites ruled the land, to the present century and the continuing tension between the Israelis and Palestinians, Jerusalem has always constituted the greatest prize. A glimpse into Jerusalem's history can shed some light on the complexities that still exist to this day.

According to the Bible, in 1004 BC, King David conquered Jerusalem, declaring it his capital and naming it The City of David (*see p46*). David's son, Solomon, is attributed with having built the First Temple, but following his death the kingdom split into two kingdoms, those of Israel and Judah, the latter retaining Jerusalem as its capital. In 586 BC, Jerusalem fell to the Babylonians, the Temple was destroyed and the Jews fled. During the succeeding Persian rulers, the Jews returned, built the Second Temple and restored Jerusalem to a centre of religious activity. Over the following centuries, Jerusalem changed hands, going from Alexander the Great to Syrian Seleucid rule (under which the Second Temple was destroyed) to a period of Jewish independence.

In 63 BC, the Romans conquered Jerusalem and Herod became king; he embarked on a massive phase of construction. Following his death, Roman rule became more heavy-handed and eventually led to revolts by the Jews, who were ultimately expelled and the city burnt to the ground.

Constantine brought Christianity to the pagan city in the 4th century, and over the next three centuries, churches were built, pilgrims flocked to the holy sites and Jerusalem became the single-most important Christian city in the world. In AD 638, however, the city was conquered by the Arab Islamic Empire, and over the following 400 years, Muslims, Christians and Jews lived and practised their faiths alongside one another. It was during this time that Jerusalem was recognised as the third-holiest place in Islam and the Dome of the Rock built (*see p39*).

The 11th century saw the advent of the Crusaders; they came to 'free' Jerusalem from the Turks, who by now controlled the city and had expelled the Christians. Two centuries of bloody battles ensued, during which most of Jerusalem's Muslim and Jewish residents fled. In 1099, the Crusaders captured Jerusalem and declared it capital of the Latin Kingdom of Jerusalem. It eventually fell to the Mamluk Saladin, who permitted the return of Muslims and Jews to the city.

By the 20th century, the Ottomans had control of Jerusalem, and the Old City had been divided into the quarters we see today. When the empire collapsed and Jerusalem was swallowed up by the British Mandate, the city boomed. Throughout this time, struggles for control between Jews and Palestinians began to heighten, and tensions rose to breaking point with riots in the 1920s and the Arab Revolt between 1936 and 1939. When the British Mandate dissolved and Israel declared independence, the city found itself at the heart of the 1948 Arab–Israeli War. By the end of the war, the city was divided, with Jordan controlling East Jerusalem and the Old City, and Israel the west. It wasn't until the 1967 Six-Day War that Israeli forces united the two sides.

Israel's declaration of Jerusalem as its capital is a controversial one, and not recognised by the UN or much of the international community. Today, each religious group is given free rein to govern its religious sites, but tensions remain high and the peaceful balance in the Holy City ever fragile.

Mount of Olives – one of Jerusalem's many holy sites

CITY CENTRE AND EAST JERUSALEM
Garden Tomb

Believed by some to be the site of the tomb of Joseph of Arimathea, and therefore the place of Jesus' resurrection, it is a far cry from the Church of the Holy Sepulchre (the other contender for the site of Golgotha). Here at the site in East Jerusalem, just north of the Damascus Gate, quiet prayer gardens allow for contemplation and worship, frequented by pilgrim groups who sit under the shady trees. Also of interest here is a large water cistern dating from pre-Christian times. It is the third largest discovered in Jerusalem.

Conrad Schik St. Tel: (02) 627 2745. www.gardentomb.com. Open: Mon–Sat 9am–noon & 2–5.30pm. Free admission.

German Colony

Built by the German Templars in the 1800s, the neighbourhood is today a quaint, leafy suburb and one of the trendiest places in the city. Centring on Emek Refaim Street, it is awash with cool cafés, each with their own shady, cobbled patios, modern restaurants and hugely sought-after apartments.
Emek Refaim St.

Great Synagogue

Undoubtedly Israel's finest and grandest synagogue, it was built to reflect the architectural style of the First Temple and contains some beautiful stained-glass windows. It was built in 1982 and was dedicated to the six million Jews who perished in the Holocaust. Today, it acts as a centre of worship, study, culture and social interaction for Jews from across the world.
56 King George V St. Tel: (02) 623 0628. www.jerusalemgreatsynagogue.com. Open: daily 9am–noon. Free admission.

Israel Museum

Housing some of the country's – and indeed world's – finest exhibits and artefacts, the Israel Museum is an excellent way to put the complex history into context. In their own wing, the Dead Sea Scrolls are displayed in an exhibition that follows their discovery

The Great Synagogue

Extraordinary architecture at the Israel Museum

along the Dead Sea shore at Qumran (*see p123*); while Judaica from across the world, art pieces from renowned artists, ethnographic displays, a vast and detailed model of the Second Temple, and the new archaeology wing featuring artefacts from all of the country's phases of occupation are but some of the displays on offer.
Ruppin Rd. Tel: (02) 670 8811. www.imj.org.il. Open: Sun, Mon, Wed, Thur & Sat 10am–5pm, Tue 4–9pm, Fri 10am–2pm. Admission charge.

Knesset

Located in the imposing-looking building in the heart of Jerusalem's new city is the Knesset, the seat of Israel's parliament. While solo entry is obviously not permitted, guided tours are offered for those wishing to understand more about the political make-up of this complex country as well as gain insight into the culture, history and religions. Modest dress is required and guided tours should be booked in advance.

Rothschild St. Tel: (02) 675 3420.
www.knesset.gov.il. Tours: Sun & Thur
8.30am, noon & 2pm. Free admission.

Me'a She'arim

One of Jerusalem's most intriguing neighbourhoods is ultra-Orthodox Me'a She'arim. As though entering a bygone era, visitors will undoubtedly find this a unique place, where traditional Jewish dress is worn without exception, where Yiddish – not Hebrew – is spoken, and where an ambience of religious learning permeates the air. Signs warn visitors to heed the religious laws, and it is inadvisable to enter during Shabbat hours. Modest dress is mandatory (including long skirts for women, not trousers) as well as the covering of arms and chests. Refrain from displays of affection and do not touch any of the residents; women in particular should not touch men.

Rockefeller Museum

A branch of the Israel Museum located in East Jerusalem, this makes a perfect accompaniment to visits to Israel's countless impressive and historically significant archaeological sites. Finds excavated from Caesarea (*see pp83–5*), Akko (*see pp78–83*), Beit She'an (*see pp92–3*), the Church of the Holy Sepulchre (*see pp35–6*) and the Al-Aqsa Mosque (*see p39*) are on display, and the thousands of finds are exhibited in chronological order.
Sultan Suleiman St. Tel: (02) 670 8011.

OSKAR SCHINDLER

Throughout World War II, much of Europe turned a blind eye as their Jewish neighbours were placed in ghettos and eventually murdered. Yet a few risked their lives to help, and today these people are listed and honoured as 'Righteous Amongst the Nations'. Within that list is one Nazi: Oskar Schindler. His story was made famous by Stephen Spielberg's Hollywood film which depicts the extents to which Schindler, a factory owner, went in order to save the several hundred Jews that worked for him. After the war, Schindler was ostracised from his homeland, broke and devastated. Upon his death in 1974, his coffin was paraded through the streets of Jerusalem and buried, at his request, in the Catholic cemetery on Mount Zion.

www.imj.org.il. Open: Sun, Mon, Wed &
Thur 10am–3pm, Sat 10am–2pm.
Free admission.

Shuk Mahane Yehuda (Mahane Yehuda Market)

For an authentic Jerusalem experience, it doesn't come better than the hubbub, crowds, scents and tastes of the Mahane Yehuda Market. It sells everything from fresh fruit and vegetables, spices and olives, meats and fish to home items and clothes, and come Friday morning, the place is shoulder-to-shoulder as residents prepare for Shabbat. Nestled amid the countless stalls are small, rustic eateries, with Middle Eastern dishes and traditional home cooking that have long made them some of the best eating spots in the city.
Mahane Yehuda neighbourhood. Open:
Sun–Thur 9am–8pm, Fri 9am–Shabbat.

Yad Vashem (Holocaust Memorial Museum)

In a country where the horrific and devastating Holocaust (*Shoah* in Hebrew) is still vivid, Yad Vashem has become a source of remembrance, where chilling displays portray the horror of one of the world's worst cases of genocide (*see pp50–51*). The long museum complex is designed as a walk-through of the events leading up to and during the Holocaust, and displays are frank, moving and, in some places, disturbing. Yet it is a crucially important episode in Jewish history and that of many Israelis. A garden of remembrance provides a peaceful contrast to the museum, while the new **Central Database of Shoah Victims' Names** is now housed within a circular hall lined with the faces of those who died.

Herzl Boulevard. Tel: (02) 644 3420. www.yadvashem.org. Open: Sun–Wed 9am–5pm, Thur 9am–8pm, Fri 9am–2pm. Free admission (under 10s not allowed). Bus: 13, 16–18, 20–27.

A poignant exhibit at the Holocaust Museum

MOUNT OF OLIVES
Church of All Nations and the Garden of Gethsemane

With its brightly painted façade and prime location at the foot of the Mount of Olives just opposite the Old City, the **Church of all Nations** is hard to miss, especially as it sits among the ancient, gnarled olive trees that adorn the **Garden of Gethsemane**, known in Christian tradition as the site of Jesus' agony, prayer, betrayal by Judas and arrest. Within the church, the Rock of Agony is believed to be the stone where Jesus prayed.

Jericho Rd. Tel: (02) 628 3264. Open: daily 8.30am–noon & 2–5.30pm. Free admission.

The Garden of Gethsemane

City of David

Excavations here revealed one of the most significant finds in Jerusalem's history: the 3,000-year-old city of Jerusalem as it was first built by King David to unite the tribes of Israel. Today, the site is a busy and well-developed slice of history, with an archaeological park, a (rather wet) tour of Hezekiah's Tunnel and a 3-D movie being a few of the highlights.

Kidron Valley. Tel: (02) 626 2341. www.cityofdavid.org.il. Open: Sun–Thur 8am–7pm, Fri 8am–2pm. Admission charge.

Dome of the Ascension

One of the contenders for the Christian site of Jesus' ascension, it is also worshipped by Muslims, who recognise Jesus as a prophet, and today it is the site of a small, octagonal-shaped mosque. A church once stood here, but it was destroyed by Saladin in 1187.

Open: mornings, although hours vary, so ring the doorbell to gain entry. Admission charge.

Mary Magdalene Church

Built as a gift in 1888 by Tsar Alexander III for his mother, the Grand Duchess Elizabeth Fyodorovna, the traditional Russian architecture of the church's golden onion domes are unmistakable. Elizabeth was killed by the Bolsheviks in 1918 and her body buried within her beloved church. Also interred within the church is Princess Alice of Battenberg, the Grand Duchess's niece

Mary Magdalene Church and the Mount of Olives Cemetery

Hebrew, and former Prime Minister Menachem Begin.

Jericho Rd. Cemetery open: Sun–Thur 8am–4pm, Fri 3am–1pm. Visitors centre open: Sun–Thur 9am–5pm. Tel: (02) 627 5050. Free admission.

Tomb of the Virgin Mary

A wide marble staircase, ornately decorated with hanging lanterns and beautiful Greek Orthodox religious artefacts, leads down to a large, dark church that commemorates the burial of Jesus' mother, Mary. Alongside the tomb is a Muslim prayer niche, since the site is recorded within Islam as being the place above which Muhammad saw a light shine over Mary's tomb on his Night Journey from Mecca.

Jericho Rd. Open: daily 6am–12.30pm & 2–6pm. Free admission.

and mother of Prince Philip, Duke of Edinburgh, who followed in her aunt's footsteps by dedicating her life to God and helping those in need.

Raba El-Adawaiyeh St. Tel: (02) 628 4371. Open: Tue–Thur 10am–noon. Free admission.

Mount of Olives Cemetery

Sprawling across the southern slopes of the Mount of Olives, the Jewish cemetery is considered prime real estate, and many Jews aspire to be buried here, for Judaism dictates that when the Messiah comes, the resurrection of the dead will begin here. The cemetery has been used for over 3,000 years, except between the years 1948 and 1967 when the city was divided. Notable graves include Eliezer Ben Yehuda, who is accredited with reinventing modern

Mount of Olives Cemetery

OUTER JERUSALEM
Ammunition Hill

This was the site of one of the 1967 Six-Day War's deadliest battles and today acts as a memorial for all the fallen soldiers of Israel's many wars. Tunnels and bunkers have been left in situ, and the site is often frequented by groups of uniform-clad new recruits who come to pay their respects to the fallen.

Givat HaTachmoshet. Tel: (02) 582 8442.
www.givathatachmosht.org.il.
Open: Sun–Thur 9am–6pm, Fri
9am–2pm. Admission charge.
Bus: 4, 9, 25, 28.

Ein Kerem

The delightful little neighbourhood on Jerusalem's outskirts is a breath of fresh air after the bustle of the city. Gentle green hills, olive groves and, in spring, the sweet scent of blossom surround the quaint little village in which are located the **Church of St John** (built to commemorate the birth of John the Baptist), the **Church of the Visitation** (commemorating Mary visiting Elizabeth) and **Mary's Spring** (where, according to biblical tradition, Mary and Elizabeth met). Several delightful little restaurants and cafés, plus an

Ein Kerem's Church of the Visitation

artist's quarter, make for a pleasant day trip.

Church of St John. Tel: (02) 632 3000. Open: daily 8am–noon & 2.30–6pm. Free admission. Church of the Visitation. Open: daily 8.30am–noon & 2.30–6pm. Free admission. Bus: 17 & 17a (from the central bus station).

Jerusalem Biblical Zoo

Part of a nationwide conservation project to preserve the animals that once roamed the land in biblical times, the zoo makes for a lovely family outing. Animals include exotic species such as elephants, lions, monkeys and cheetah, as well as birds, reptiles, fish and amphibians.

Malha neighbourhood. Tel: (02) 675 0111. www.jerusalemzoo.org.il. Open: Sun–Thur 9am–5pm, Fri 9am–4.30pm, Sat 10am–5pm. Admission charge. The train stops outside the zoo and all buses heading to Malha Train Station will get you near.

Mini Israel

Located on Route 1 between Jerusalem and Tel Aviv is the kitsch yet interesting Mini Israel park. As the name suggests, the park is comprised of technically accurate models of some of Israel's most famous landmarks, including Jerusalem's Old City, Tel Aviv and Haifa, all built at a scale of 1:25.

Latrun. Tel: (08) 913 0000/10. www.minisrael.co.il. Open: summer Sat–Thur 10am–10pm, winter Sat–Thur 10am–5pm. Admission charge.

THE MAKING OF A PRIME MINISTER

David Ben Gurion (1886–1973) was born in Poland to Zionist parents and, at the age of 20, arrived in the Holy Land and became active in Zionist circles. Throughout the late Ottoman period and during the British Mandate, Ben Gurion was a member of the Socialist-Zionist group and then of the Jewish Legion. He was a founder of trade unions and a representative in the World Zionist Organization and Jewish Agency. Having been at the forefront of the battle to create the State of Israel, Ben Gurion signed the declaration of independence on 14 May 1948, and shortly after became the new country's first elected prime minister.

Soreq Caves Nature Reserve

Also located on Route 1 between Tel Aviv and Jerusalem (about 12km (7½ miles) away from Jerusalem) and not far from Ben Gurion International Airport is this series of caves containing some of the most impressive stalactites in the world. The caves were discovered in 1968 when nearby quarrying unearthed the maze of stunning caves and their stalactites, believed by scientists to be five million years old. The formations are incredibly beautiful, and wandering through the illuminated caves feels like walking through an alien world. Guided tours allow you to fully understand the ancient geological process that created the phenomenon.

Near Beit Shemesh. Tel: (02) 991 5756. www.parks.org.il. Open: daily 8am–5pm. Admission charge. Bus: 415 & 417 (from Jerusalem to Beit Shemesh, 2km/1¼ miles from cave entrance).

In memory of the Holocaust

The Holocaust is a word that evokes emotion the world over, but nowhere more so than in the State of Israel. The wounds are still raw in a country where most people's parents or grandparents were affected in some way by the genocide that saw two-thirds of Europe's Jews perish.

The Nazis came to power in Germany in 1933 and held as their core belief that they were racially superior and that the Jews, among others, were a threat to their ideals. At the time they came into power, there were approximately nine million Jews in Europe, mainly in countries which Nazi Germany would occupy during the course of World War II. By the end of the war, the Nazis had killed around six million of Europe's Jews, as well as millions of others, including homosexuals, Roma (gypsies), the disabled, Jehovah's Witnesses, Soviets and Communists, as part of their 'Final Solution'. Through the creation of concentration camps throughout Germany and Poland, millions of people were removed from city ghettos and gassed.

In the aftermath of the Holocaust – Greek for 'sacrifice by fire' – survivors found themselves alone, the world they once knew and so many in it having been lost forever. Between 1948 and 1951, 136,000 European Jews emigrated to Israel. Others fled to the United States and other countries, and by 1957 many of the Jewish communities in Europe had disappeared.

Today in Israel, the Holocaust remains a sensitive topic, the decades having done little to heal the wounds inflicted on a faith, a culture and its people. Remembrance of the event is paramount and Holocaust Memorial Day (*see p24*) is a hugely important event in the Israeli calendar. The day is a national holiday, and the entire

YAD VASHEM

In 2005, Jerusalem's new Yad Vashem Holocaust Memorial Museum (*see p45*) was inaugurated and its opening attended by dozens of heads of state. Free to the public, it aims to share with the world the almost total devastation of the Jewish people, and its displays are as moving as they are shocking. Rooms full of shoes, hair and clothes are chilling, while the chronological timetable of events leading up to the Holocaust provides some necessary background. At the end of the museum is the Hall of Names, where faces of those who died line the domed ceiling. Relatives can search for ancestors in a database that was created in order to give a name to each of the millions who perished.

country closes in respect for its ancestors, families and comrades who perished. Television stations show documentaries and films on the Holocaust; as difficult as most find to watch them, it is held to be important that the younger generations should fully understand the horror of what happened. The religious pray, families gather and an atmosphere of sorrow and passion permeates. Indeed, as the clock strikes at 11am, every person in the country stops for a two-minute silence. As though the pause button has been pressed, vehicles grind to a halt on the motorways and their drivers emerge, pedestrians stop in the middle of zebra crossings, and a hush blankets the land.

A haunting display of photographs at the Holocaust Museum

Walk: Via Dolorosa

Every Friday, hundreds of Christians begin a slow procession through the winding streets of Jerusalem's Old City as a sign of remembrance and sorrow for Jesus as he walked to his crucifixion. Since early Christian times, thousands of pilgrims have come to Jerusalem to undertake this ceremonial walk. There are 14 stations along the Via Dolorosa – which translates as 'Path of Sorrow' – each commemorating events that occurred as Jesus walked to Golgotha (in the Church of the Holy Sepulchre).

The walk is 500m (550yds) and takes approximately one hour allowing for stops at each station.

Begin at Station I, at the Madrasa Al-Omariya, located just outside the Temple Mount, 300m (330yds) from Lion's Gate.

1 Station I

The site where Pontius Pilate condemned Jesus to death is believed to be located beneath the Madrasa Al-Omariya (*Open: Mon–Thur & Sat 2.30–6pm, Fri 2.30–4pm. Free admission*).
Located directly opposite Station I is Station II.

2 Station II

This is where Jesus took up his cross, an act commemorated by the Monastery of the Flagellation (*Open: daily 8–11.45am & 2–6pm. Free admission*). Stained-glass windows portray Pontius Pilate flogging Jesus and placing the crown of thorns on his head.
Turn left into the Muslim Quarter souk at the corner of Via Dolorosa and El-Wad Street. Immediately on the left is a chapel marking Station III.

3 Station III

Station III commemorates Jesus falling for the first time under the weight of the cross.
A short distance (20m/22yds) along El-Wad Street is Station IV.

4 Station IV

This is the site where, according to tradition, Jesus met his mother, Mary. A small Armenian church marks the spot.
Station V is located on the right, where El-Wad Street meets Via Dolorosa again.

5 Station V

A small Franciscan oratory stands on the site where Simon of Cyrene was made by Roman soldiers to help Jesus carry the cross.
Follow the lane uphill until you come to Station VI.

6 Station VI

The Convent of the Little Sisters of Jesus was built over the site believed to be the house of Veronica who, according to the Gospels, wiped Jesus' brow.

Station VII is on the corner where Souk Khan es-Zeit Street and El-Khanqa Street meet.

7 Station VII

A Franciscan chapel marks the place where Jesus fell a second time.

30m (33yds) further along El-Khanqa Street is a plaque marking Station VIII.

8 Station VIII

It was here that Jesus told the daughter of Jerusalem not to weep for him.

Turn around and walk back to Souk Khan es-Zeit Street and turn right. A stairway 50m (55yds) on leads to a chapel in which you will find Station IX.

9 Station IX

Within the chapel is a Roman column where Jesus fell for the third time.

Go down Souq Khan es-Zeit, and at the end turn right into Souq Al-Dabbagha. Stations X–XIV are located inside the Church of the Holy Sepulchre.

10 Stations X–XIV

These stations mark the sites where Jesus was stripped, crucified, died on the cross, was laid in the tomb and was resurrected.

Return to the Temple Mount via the same route you came.

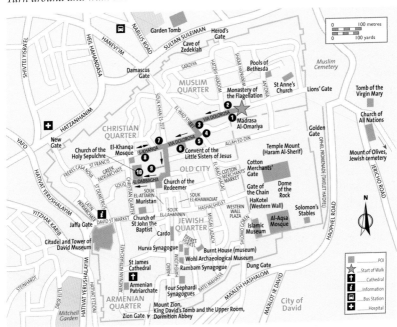

Tel Aviv-Jaffa

Located on the Mediterranean Sea, with a wide strip of golden, sandy beaches fringing it, Tel Aviv is a vibrant, fun-loving city boasting hundreds of bars, cafés and restaurants which are busy until the small hours even in the middle of the week. The city is home to world-class museums, art galleries, theatres and orchestras, and it exudes a laid-back atmosphere like no other Israeli city.

While few would describe Tel Aviv as beautiful, its collection of buildings constructed in the Bauhaus architectural style has been awarded UNESCO World Heritage status, and its long, tree-lined boulevards, big green parks and seafront promenade are undoubtedly charming. Offering a thoroughly secular lifestyle, new buildings and a thriving social life, modern Tel Aviv stands as a complete and, for some, refreshing contrast to Jerusalem.

Apart from its obvious appeal for socialites, Tel Aviv is also the economic, commercial and transport hub of the country. Jerusalem's disputed status as capital city has seen Tel Aviv fulfil the role of administrative capital, most notably with regards to the foreign embassies and consulates which reside here.

Just along the coast from Tel Aviv, the ancient port city of Jaffa is today a delightful suburb of the modern city. Cobbled lanes and stone buildings form the picturesque Old City of Jaffa, and the streets are abuzz with cars and daily activity, and Arab life and culture prevail.

Tel Aviv city centre
Azrieli Center
Towering above the city are the three skyscrapers known as the Azrieli Center. The square, triangular and round buildings are especially attractive at night when they are totally illuminated. At their highest, the buildings measure 187m (613ft), and an **observatory** (and 3-D film about the city) is located on the 49th floor of

The towering Azrieli Center

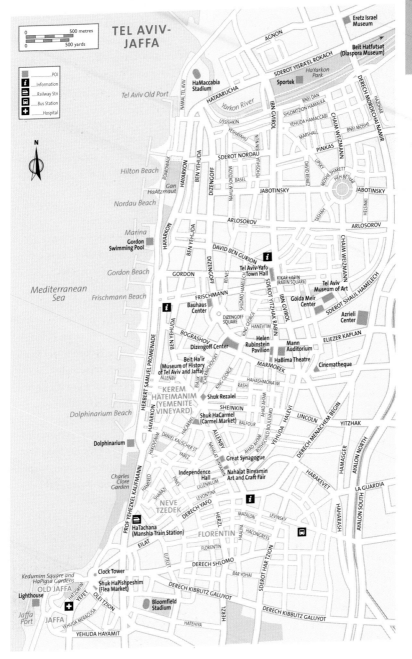

TEL AVIV-JAFFA

0	500 metres
0	500 yards

POI
Information
Railway Stn
Bus Station
Hospital

N

Eretz Israel Museum

Beit Hatfutsot (Diaspora Museum)

AGNON

SDEROT YISRA'EL ROKACH

HaYarkon Park

Sportek

Tel Aviv Old Port

HaMaccabia Stadium

HATAARUCHA

Yarkon River

BNEI DAN

SHLOMTZION HAMALKA

YEHUDA HAMACCABI

CHAIM WEIZMANN

BNEI MOSHE

DERECH MORDECHAI NAMIR

HADAR

USSISHKIN

MARSHALL

PINKAS

YESHAYAHU

SDEROT NORDAU

YEHOSHUA

NAHUM SOKOLOW

BASEL

LIPSKY

DAVID REMEZ

MOSHE SHARETT

HEH BE'IYAR

Hilton Beach

BEN YEHUDA

DIZENGOFF

JABOTINSKY

JABOTINSKY

Gan HaAtzmaut

Nordau Beach

ARLOSOROV

ARLOSOROV

TAGAH

HEH BESIVAN

Marina

Gordon Swimming Pool

HAYARKON

BEN YEHUDA

DIZENGOFF

DAVID BEN GURION

CHAIM WEIZMANN

Gordon Beach

GORDON

REINES

Tel Aviv-Yafo Town Hall

KIKAR RABIN (RABIN SQUARE)

Tel Aviv Museum of Art

SDEROT YITZHAK RABIN

IBN GVIROL

Golda Meir Center

SDEROT SHAUL HAMELECH

Mediterranean Sea

Frischmann Beach

FRISCHMANN

Bauhaus Center

SHLOMO HAMELECH

KING GEORGE

HANEVI'IM

Azrieli Center

ELIEZER KAPLAN

DIZENGOFF SQUARE

BOGRASHOV

Dizengoff Center

Helen Rubinstein Pavilion

Mann Auditorium

HERBERT SAMUEL PROMENADE

BEN YEHUDA

Beit Ha'ir (Museum of History of Tel Aviv and Jaffa)

BILIK

TCHERNICHOVSKY

KING GEORGE

MARMOREK

HaBima Theatre

Cinematheque

HAYARKON

ALLENBY

RASHI

HASHAHMONA'IM

AHAD HA'AM

YEHUDA HALEVI

LINCOLN

DERECH MENACHEM BEGIN

YITZHAK

KEREM HATEIMANIM (YEMENITE VINEYARD)

Shuk Rezalel

SHEINKIN

Shuk HaCarmel (Carmel Market)

BALFOUR

AHAD HA'AM

ROTHSCHILD BOULEVARD

HAMASGER

AVALON NORTH

Dolphinarium Beach

HACARMEL

HACOVSHIM

DANIEL KALISCHER ST

YABEZ

ALLENBY

NAHALAT BINYAMIN

Great Synagogue

HARAKEVET

LA GUARDIA

Dolphinarium

Charles Clore Garden

PROF. YEHEZKEL KAUFMANN

HAKEVED

SHABAZI

PINES

Independence Hall

Nahalat Binyamin Art and Craft Fair

LILLENBLUM

LEVONTINE

HERZL

AVALON SOUTH

HAHARASH

NEVE TZEDEK

DERECH YAFO

MATALON

LEVINSKY

HaTachana (Manshia Train Station)

EILAT

HALIYA

HACONGRESS

FLORENTIN

FLORENTIN

EIFELET

DERECH SHLOMO

BAR YOHAI

Kedumim Square and HaPisga Gardens

OLD JAFFA

Lighthouse

Clock Tower

Shuk HaPishpeshim (Flea Market)

DERECH KIBBUTZ GALUYOT

HERZL

DERECH KIBBUTZ GALUYOT

YEFET

OLEI TZION

Bloomfield Stadium

HATEHIYA

Jaffa Port

JAFFA

YEHUDA MERAGUSA

YEHUDA HAYAMIT

Bauhaus architectural detail

the Circular Tower, providing a bird's-eye view of the city as far as the Mediterranean Sea. A gourmet restaurant is located on the same floor.

While the majority of the buildings' space is dedicated to offices, the entire lower portion of the complex contains a shopping centre. The city's biggest fashion mall is chock-full of mid-range, higher-end and designer shops and is a glitzy contrast to the dated Dizengoff Center.

Azrieli Center. 123 Menachem Begin St. Tel: (03) 608 1179. www.azrielicenter. co.il. Open: Sun–Thur 10am–10pm, Fri 9.30am–5pm, Sat 8pm–11pm. Azrieli Observatory. 49th floor, Circular Tower. Tel: (03) 608 1179. Open: summer Sat–Thur 9.30am–8pm, Fri 9.30am–6pm; winter daily 9.30am–6pm. Admission charge.

Bauhaus Center

Since it was awarded UNESCO World Heritage status based on its number of buildings of Bauhaus architecture, Tel Aviv has seen a huge increase in interest in this minimalist, simple style. In a city that embraces the arts so strongly, it is probably unsurprising that the Bauhaus Center has become a popular addition to the scene. The centre is just a small shop located on Dizengoff Street, but it sells books, art, postcards and souvenirs as well as offering exhibits, guided tours or audio guides.

99 Dizengoff St. Tel: (03) 522 0249. www.bauhaus-center.com. Open: Sun–Thur 10am–7.30pm, Fri 10am–2.30pm, Sat noon–7.30pm. Free admission.

Beit Ha'ir (Museum of History of Tel Aviv and Jaffa)

Located in the city's old town hall, the museum is a new addition to Tel Aviv's cultural scene. The beautifully renovated building contains displays on the history of the city, from its founding to the present day. Photography exhibits, a reconstruction of Meir Dizengoff's office, a historical timeline and documentary films are among the varied exhibits.

27 Bialik St. Tel: (03) 525 3403. Open: Mon–Thur 9am–5pm, Fri & Sat 10am–2pm. Admission charge.

Dizengoff area

Much more than just a shopping centre, the **Dizengoff Center** has become an icon of the city. The somewhat old-fashioned maze of walkways and stairs is 1980s architecture at its most eccentric. The centre is constantly full, a stream of families, soldiers, young couples and giggling teenagers finding something to entertain them, whether they're interested in high-street shops and cafés, cinemas or sports and toy shops. Every Friday morning a food market comes to the centre; vendors set up stalls along the walkways, selling excellent cheap dishes. The place gets extremely crowded, so get there early and hungry.

Just outside the shopping centre is **Dizengoff Street**, one of the main roads running through the city. It runs perpendicular to the seafront, from the centre at its southern end to HaYarkon

Park at its northern. A hubbub of traffic, buses and pedestrians pours along at all times of the day and night, and the pavements are lined with street artisans, cheap eateries, colourful juice bars and rather a lot of gaudy wedding dress shops.

Just along from the shopping centre is **Dizengoff Square**, with another piece of 1980s architecture in its centre in the form of a musical fountain. A cinema complex stands on one side of the square, while on the other several boutique hotels have appeared in more recent years.

While few would describe the Dizengoff area as beautiful, or even charming, it is undoubtedly an integral part of everyday Tel Aviv life and a trip to the city would be incomplete without a visit.

Dizengoff Center. Corner of Dizengoff & King George sts. Tel: (03) 621 2416. www.dizengoff-center.co.il. Open: Sun–Thur 9am–midnight, Fri 9am–4pm, Sat 8pm–midnight.

Kikar Rabin (Rabin Square)

Located in the heart of the city, Rabin Square has been the setting for many a dramatic event in Israel's recent history. This is where passionate Israelis come to rejoice in Independence Day celebrations, protest at political rallies, let their hair down for Gay Pride or dance at concerts. The most infamous event to have occurred on this ground, however, was the assassination of Prime Minister Yitzhak Rabin on 5 November

Retail therapy on Dizengoff Street

Rabin Square

1995. It was during a peace rally attended by thousands that the prime minister was shot by a Jewish student, Yigal Amir. The country was shocked to its core by the assassination, and to this day it is a sensitive subject. A memorial stands at the north end of the square.

For most of the year, however, Rabin Square is a relaxed place where Tel Avivians come to play frisbee, walk their dogs, exhibit art or simply sit among the pigeons. It is bordered by the rather unsightly town hall at its northern end, and the busy restaurant- and café-lined Ibn Gvirol Street to its east.

Tel Aviv Museum of Art

In a city so proud of its artistic flair and heritage, the Tel Aviv Museum of Art stands as the showpiece. The museum opened its doors in 1932 in the home of Tel Aviv's first mayor, Meir Dizengoff (see 'Rothschild Boulevard' listing, pp60–61), and moved to its current location within this impressive cultural

complex in 1971. Modern and contemporary 20th-century art is displayed in a series of permanent and temporary exhibits that include painting, sculpture, drawings, photography, architecture and design elements by world-renowned artists.

Within the complex is the **Helena Rubenstein Pavilion for Contemporary Art**, which displays works by Israeli and up-and-coming young artists and has become well respected in its own right.

27 Shaul HaMelech Boulevard. Tel: (03) 607 7020. www.tamuseum.com. Open: Mon, Wed & Sat 10am–4pm, Tue & Thur 10am–10pm. Admission charge.

Installation at the Tel Aviv Museum of Art

South Tel Aviv

HaTachana (Manshia Train Station)

After five years of careful renovations, HaTachana opened to the public in 2010. The train station is the city's oldest, and formed a crucial line between the port city of Jaffa and Jerusalem during the Ottoman period. The complex has today been restored to its former glory and now hosts galleries, weekly markets, jazz concerts, art exhibitions and festivals. Boutiques and cafés add even more charm and it has quickly become one of Tel Aviv's hottest new spots.

Tel: (03) 609 995. Open: Sat–Thur 10am–10pm, Fri 10am–5pm. Free admission.

Kerem HaTeimanim

In a busy, noisy, secular city, Kerem HaTeimanim ('Yemenite Vineyard') provides a respite from the hubbub. Founded in 1902 by Yemenite Jews, it has long been known as one of the most religiously observant areas of the city, tucked away behind the bustling Carmel Market (*see p61*). For years it was a rather run-down neighbourhood, with crumbling buildings and narrow, unkempt streets. Over recent years, however, the area has become one of the trendiest parts of the city in which to live, and property prices have soared. Traditional Yemenite restaurants are nestled away among the cobbled streets, bougainvillea plants wind their way up the fronts of balconied buildings, and an air of religious adherence permeates.

Bohemian Neve Tzedek

Nahalat Binyamin Art and Craft Fair

This much-loved artists' fair sees all manner of artists and artisans set up stalls twice a week and display their handicrafts. Competition is high to have a stall here, and artists must apply to the city council, which selects the lucky winners. What makes the market particularly unique is that the artists create their works on their stalls, allowing the general public to watch. Offering everything from paintings to ceramics, from unique toys to clocks made from glass beer bottles, it is a treasure trove of interest and a great place to pick up souvenirs and presents. To add to the light-hearted, bohemian feel, clowns, fortune-tellers and performers strut their stuff and delight the crowds.

Nahalat Binyamin Street. Open: Tue & Fri 10am–5pm.

Neve Tzedek

This neighbourhood was the first to appear outside the old Jaffa city walls in

1887 and is as such Tel Aviv's oldest neighbourhood. Throughout the years it slowly declined until, during the 1980s, the Tel Aviv Municipality performed a major renovation and overhaul of the area. Today, it is one of the city's most charming neighbourhoods and certainly worth a visit. Artists and artisans, the Suzanne Dellal Dance Centre, art galleries, and shops selling jewellery, designer clothes and pottery have made this their home, creating a chic yet bohemian vibe. With countless cafés and restaurants added to the mix, this is a charming place to spend an afternoon.

Rothschild Boulevard

Few would describe Tel Aviv as a beautiful city. Yet, if there is one area that stands as an exception to this view, it would be the tree-lined Rothschild Boulevard. Running

Promenading on Rothschild Boulevard

BEN GURION

Throughout his almost 20 years as premier, Israel's first prime minister, David Ben Gurion, led Israel to victory in the 1948 Arab–Israeli War and the 1956 Sinai War, encouraged vast Jewish immigration from around the world, oversaw the airlifting of hundreds of Jews out of Arab countries, instigated the building of countless towns and villages, and developed Israel's infrastructure. He was also a strong advocator of tapping into the resources of the desert lands, and upon his retirement, he and his wife, Paula, moved to the remote kibbutz of Sde Boker (*see pp121–2*), where they were later buried.

from the city centre to the Neve Tzedek neighbourhood, the wide boulevard has at its core a pedestrianised walkway, where young mothers push babies in prams, dog-walkers stretch the legs of their packs of pooches and Tel Avivians nibble on sandwiches from the kiosks that dot the walkway. Come the weekend and the boulevard is the place to see and to be seen. The cafés and restaurants that line the pavements are filled to capacity, musicians entertain the crowds who relax on the grassy central walkway, and children play in the playgrounds. To add to its appeal, Rothschild Boulevard is also home to countless buildings of the Bauhaus architectural style for which Tel Aviv was awarded UNESCO heritage status (*see p62*). In addition, the street also houses **Independence Hall**, in which Israel's declaration of independence was signed on 14 May 1948. The room where the event took place has been left exactly as it was on that day, with

Fresh fruit for sale on Sheinkin Street

television cameras, furniture and flags still in place. The residence later became the home of the city's first mayor, Meir Dizengoff, and afterwards housed the Tel Aviv Museum of Art until its move to its current location (*see p58*).
Independence Hall. 16 Rothschild Boulevard. Tel: (03) 517 3942. Open: Sun–Fri 9am–2pm. Admission charge.

Sheinkin Street

Flanked by one-off boutiques, shoe shops, cafés, juice bars and tattoo parlours, Sheinkin Street has long attracted the 'in' crowd. At weekends, the street is a hive of activity and you will be hard-pressed to find a seat in any street-side café. Musicians play in the little square, artisans sell jewellery, stands selling fresh fruit juice adorn the pavements, and the city's trendy young residents come to mingle and shop.

Shuk HaCarmel (Carmel Market)

In a city where museums, architecture, superb restaurants and trendy cafés dominate, the Carmel Market represents traditional Tel Aviv and is a must-see on a visit to the city. Squeezed into the long, covered market are dozens of stalls, leading from Allenby Street at the top to Daniel Kalischer Street at the bottom. Fruit and vegetables, olives and spices, baked goods, clothes, household items, toys and sweets battle for space among the crowds who come to take advantage of the fresh produce. Just off the main market street are little bakeries selling sticky, sweet baklava and pastries.
Open: Sun–Thur 9.30am–5.30pm.

Walk: Beaches and Bauhaus

Tel Aviv does not have the beauty and historical magnificence of Jerusalem, but then it doesn't really care. For the city exudes its own charisma, and nowhere is this more obvious than in its Bauhaus architecture and wide, golden beaches. A long, but rewarding, walk along the city's boulevard and down the length of the seafront promenade provides a glimpse not only into Tel Aviv's pretty side, but also into the eclectic population that calls it home.

The walk is approximately 4km (2½ miles) long and takes one hour of straight walking.

Starting at the HaBima Theatre, head south down the tree-lined Rothschild Boulevard.

1 Rothschild Boulevard

A central reservation dotted with sandwich bars, play parks and shaded benches turns from tranquil to trendy at weekends, when the street is packed with young Tel Avivans. Many of the city's 4,000-plus Bauhaus buildings were constructed in the 1930s, when architects emigrated from Germany, awarding Tel Aviv the nickname 'the White City'. Indeed, in 2003, it was granted UNESCO World Heritage status for its number of Bauhaus buildings. The following numbers are all buildings of the Bauhaus style: 61, 66, 67, 73, 83, 84, 87, 89–91, 93, 99, 100, 117, 118, 119, 121, 123 and 126–128. *Rothschild Boulevard emerges into Neve*

Tzedek neighbourhood (see pp59–60). Weave through until you emerge on the seafront near the David Intercontinental Hotel. Almost directly in front is the Dolphinarium Beach.

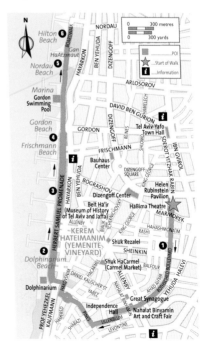

2 Dolphinarium Beach

At the city's most bohemian stretch of sand, jungle drums, fire-ball juggling, surfing, narghile pipes and impromptu guitar sessions summarise the laid-back atmosphere. There is a watersports centre and, a little further north, a popular beach bar.

Just north of the Dolphinarium Beach, the Herbert Samuel Promenade – or HaTayelet – begins.

3 Herbert Samuel Promenade

This wide pedestrian boardwalk is one of the city's best people-watching spots, as everyone – from young bronzed soldiers to the Orthodox, and from young families to the elderly – come to amble in the sunshine along the shore.

Continue walking north, up to the Frischmann and Gordon beaches.

4 Frischmann and Gordon beaches

In the centre of the city is this wide expanse of white sand. Lifeguard

Cycling along the Promenade

stations, sunbeds, toilets and cafés have made this the family favourite. On summer weekends, it is towel-to-towel, as a wonderful cross-section of society comes to enjoy the sheltered waters.

Continue north to Nordau Beach.

5 Nordau Beach

Sheltered by high hotel walls is the conservative religious beach, where Tel Aviv's more devoutly religious community comes to partake in single-sex beach days. Sundays, Tuesdays and Thursdays are for women, while Mondays, Wednesdays and Fridays are for men.

Just north of Nordau you'll find Hilton Beach.

6 Hilton Beach

Frequented by three very different groups, the beach is a great example of Tel Aviv's carefree attitude, where 'each to their own' seems to be the motto. At the far end is a dog beach, where dog owners bring their pooches down for a race along the sand. A little further along is the area known as the gay beach, where a relaxed, fun atmosphere – and plenty of tight shorts – prevails. At the southern end is a small surfing beach with some of the best breaks in the city.

To get back to your starting point, leave the seafront and cross Gan HaAtzmaut (Independence Park) and head up Nordau Street for two blocks. Turn right on to Dizengoff Street and follow it all the way back to the top of Rothschild Boulevard.

North Tel Aviv
Beit Hatfutsot (Diaspora Museum)

This once small museum has quickly risen to international acclaim as the first and largest museum dedicated to the history of the Jewish people, and in 2005 was declared by the Knesset as the national centre for Jewish communities in Israel and around the world. Through videos, drawings, reconstructions, models and computer generations, the 4,000-year-old story of the Jewish people comes to life, from both a religious and cultural standpoint. Themes and exhibits range from family and community to Zionism and politics.

Tel Aviv University. Tel: (03) 640 8000. www.bh.org.il. Open: Sun–Tue 10am–4pm, Wed & Thur 10am–8pm, Fri 9am–1pm. Admission charge.

Eretz Israel Museum

Archaeological, historical and anthropological artefacts are displayed in series of pavilions spread across the sprawling grounds of HaYarkon Park. Temporary and permanent exhibits range from glassware to coins and pottery, as well as ethnographic items and displays, Judaica and a planetarium (in Hebrew). Of particular interest are the Nechushtan pavilion, which displays a reconstruction of a Bronze Age mine, and a full reconstruction of an ancient olive press.

2 Ha'im Levanon St. Tel: (03) 641 5244. www.eretzmuseum.org.il. Open: Sun– Wed 10am–4pm, Thur 10am–8pm, Fri & Sat 10am–2pm. Admission charge.

HaYarkon Park

The city's biggest park is a green, refreshing break from the muggy

Boats on the lake in HaYarkon Park

summer heat, and locals of all ages come to picnic, ride bicycles, walk dogs and relax. The Yarkon River weaves its way through the centre of the park and a large man-made boating lake provides canoeing and boating opportunities, while for the more active sorts, football and basketball courts, table-tennis tables, a trampoline, skateboard park and climbing wall are available at the Sportek, some for free and others for an admission charge. Bicycle paths wend their way about the park and renting a bicycle is a lovely afternoon activity (but note that Israelis tend to walk on the paths rather than ride, so cycle with care). The park has also played host to several major international bands and artists who have recently, for the first time, started including Israel on their tours, and these events are attended by thousands. In summer, HaYarkon is a shoulder-to-shoulder kind of place, but there is a lively, family atmosphere and time spent here is a real highlight of a visit to the city.

Old Port

Where the Yarkon River reaches the Mediterranean Sea is Tel Aviv's Old Port. It has been many years since ships chugged in and out of the port, and when it stopped functioning as a commercial port, it quickly declined into a run-down, disused area. A major overhaul, however, has seen trendy restaurants and cafés emerge, with pumping 'pick-up' bars and big nightclubs attracting scores of partying youngsters, and a wooden promenade providing a pleasant seaside walk for those in search of a less frenetic way to spend an afternoon or evening. It is today a big part of the city's entertainment scene, and serves as a pleasant respite from the city centre on hot, humid summer days; just don't look in the direction of the unattractive power works!

Jaffa

Jaffa was twinned with Tel Aviv in recent decades, but for 4,000 years it stood alone and has seen more history than its bigger neighbour could ever attest to. Its port was once one of the Mediterranean's major trading ports and it was from here that the great trunk road to Jerusalem began. Produce from Europe, pilgrims in their thousands, Crusader soldiers and many more made their entry into the Holy Land through Jaffa's crucial port. Today, Jaffa is a bustling Arab suburb, although the Old City provides some quaint architecture and peace and quiet.

Artists' quarter

Old Jaffa charm emanates from the cobbled lanes that lead from Kedumim Square down to the port. Narrow alleyways, lined with traditional stone-built houses, create a maze and it is easy, and recommended, to simply get lost in it. Tucked away within the alleys and lanes are countless artists' galleries, whose flamboyant owners have opened their homes to allow the public to

An alleyway in the Jaffa artists' quarter

appreciate their artistry and skills as well as the architectural beauty of Jaffa's old houses. Mazal Dagim Street forms the core of the artists' quarter.

Clock Tower

The beautiful tower is one of Jaffa's iconic sights. It is the only remaining of seven clock towers built during the Ottoman period, when it was set to European time to help sea merchants arriving in the port. A free guided tour leaves from here on Wednesdays at 9.30am.

Kedumim Square and HaPigsa Gardens

In the centre of Old Jaffa is Kedumim Square, where the **History of Jaffa Museum and Visitors' Center**

(*Open: daily 10am–6pm. Admission charge*) is located. Stairs lead down to the newly renovated museum, which depicts the colourful history of the city. Around the square are the **Franciscan Church of St Peter**, which is believed to have been visited by Napoleon (hence the metal statues of him around the square), as well as the ornately decorated **Greek Orthodox Church of St Michael and St Tabitha**. On one side of the square, the cobbled alleys that form the artists' quarter lead down to the port, while on the other, **HaPigsa Gardens** (*Free admission*) are located on top of a small hill. Narrow paths weave through the pretty gardens, from the top of which is a spectacular view of the Tel Aviv coastline, and a small amphitheatre hosts summer concerts.

Port

It is difficult to imagine, as you wander around the quiet, tranquil port with its little fishing boats, piles of nets, warehouses containing art exhibits and fish restaurants, that this was once one of the world's busiest and most crucial seaports. Indeed, archaeological evidence points as far back as 4,000 years, when the Egyptians and Phoenicians used it. It is believed to be the oldest port in the world to have had uninterrupted use. Biblical accounts mention Jaffa as the route through which some building materials for King Solomon's First Temple arrived in the Holy Land, and its name has been linked with the Greeks, Peter the Apostle, the Romans, Richard the Lionheart and the Crusaders, Napoleon, Ottoman rulers and General Allenby, who conquered the city during the British Mandate period. Just beyond the sea wall are several rocks, the darkest said to be Andromeda's Rock. In Greek mythology, the beautiful Andromeda was chained to this rock by King Cepheus, her father, as a sacrifice to Poseidon's sea monster. According to legend, her brave hero came in the form of Perseus, who slayed the beast.

Shuk HaPishpeshim (Flea Market)

This market provides a true Middle Eastern experience, where colourful, traditional items are haggled for amid the busy clamour. Sale items vary widely and include brass and copper, Persian tiles and Judaica. Second-hand clothing, textiles and antique furniture add to the seemingly disorganised mish-mash of stalls. Perusing the mountains of items in search of a bargain has become a popular activity on Fridays, when the market is full to bursting, and the little cafés, restaurants and galleries that surround the market are teeming.
Open: Sun–Thur 10am–6pm, Fri 10am–2pm. Bus: 10 (from Ben Yehuda St).

Boats at rest in Jaffa Port

The party city

Tel Aviv couldn't be more different from her bigger, older, more devout sister, Jerusalem. The secular city, resting on the shores of the warm, blue waters of the Mediterranean Sea, is, in fact, not a pretty city, nor has it a particularly long history. In a country of such profound religious significance and beautiful architecture, Tel Aviv is the ugly duckling. In fact, being twinned with ancient Jaffa to its south provides it with its only historic saving grace.

Yet Tel Aviv is becoming one of the most popular and trendy cities to visit. A mere four hours' flight from Europe, the city now has budget airlines serving the new, swish Tel Aviv Ben Gurion International Airport, a seafront lined with pricey boutique hotels, and well-developed tourist facilities. For some reason, tourists are flocking to this place.

The reason is simple: atmosphere. It is true that Tel Aviv has some fabulous museums, renowned art galleries and highly respected orchestras and theatrical troupes, and these certainly add to the overall experience. Yet, it is the laid-back, comfortable, light-hearted ambience of a city that works hard during the week and plays hard at the weekend that makes people fall in love with the place. On a Friday night, when Jerusalem is shutting down for a Shabbat of prayer and religious obedience, Tel Avivians are donning their latest cool outfits bought from the likes of Sheinkin Street or the Electric Garden (Gan HaHashmal) neighbourhood, ready to hit the cafés, bars and nightclubs for which the city is so famous.

During the day and early evening, cafés are the places to be seen. Light meals and perfectly brewed coffee (Tel Avivians may be laid-back but they won't accept a poor cup of coffee) are taken while sunning on street-side tables or in shady gardens. After the sun sets (in fact not until at least 10pm), however, a move is made to the bars which, despite being hugely pricey, are jam-packed throughout the weekend. Ranging from chic wine bars to bohemian watering holes and noisy 'pick-up' bars, the city caters to every taste.

Around midnight is when the nightclubs get going, and the energetic types move on to the big dance clubs to blow off steam until the small hours. While there are many types of clubs, Israel – and Tel Aviv in particular – is well known for its pumping techno clubs, where top DJs make regular appearances.

Tel Aviv is a city that is ever changing. The best bar today will be gone tomorrow, a distant fad in the memory of fickle partygoers who have moved on to the next big thing and are willing to queue for hours to get in – even if it's just for coffee. Bars, restaurants, cafés and clubs know when they open their doors that they probably won't have many years at the top, and that's fine with them. They simply start something new. And so the evolution of Tel Aviv's famed party scene continues, in a whirr of trends, popularity, word of mouth and hints about the best parties. For whether you're a student, single, coupled up and/or homosexual, Tel Aviv undoubtedly has a party to suit you. And if it doesn't, give it six months.

Posters advertising concerts and clubs spring up all over the city

Mediterranean coast

Israel forms the eastern shore of the Mediterranean Sea, and much of the urban growth within the country has occurred in this central plain. Yet the region has been settled for centuries, and great archaeological sites, ancient port cities and Zionist colonies all found their place here. Today, these towns and cities continue to flourish, golden sands line the shore and Mount Carmel runs alongside.

Haifa is Israel's third-largest city and has a variety of attractions for the visitor; interesting museums, a busy commercial port, pretty neighbourhoods and its pièce de résistance, the Bahá'í Shrine and Gardens, provide plenty to do. Despite a devastating and violent forest fire in Mount Carmel, which saw Israel call upon the international community for aid, parts of the area are still worth visiting, most notably the quaint and picturesque town of Zichron Ya'akov. And great ancient cities, such as the ruins of Caesarea or vibrant, bustling Akko, stand on the coast as reminders of the powerful empires that conquered this land in the past, their impressive remains telling stories from the days of the Roman, Crusader and Arab rules.

In a nutshell, the Mediterranean coast is a mix of perfect beaches, historical intrigue and cosmopolitan cities, with the most developed transport network in the country, the most ideal weather and the widest range of sights and activities.

HAIFA

Israel's third-largest city doesn't profess to have the historical clout of Jerusalem nor the charisma of Tel Aviv, but it is most certainly a pleasant place to spend a few days. The city, which tumbles down the northern slope of Mount Carmel, is Israel's busiest commercial and cruise-ship port, it is the headquarters of the Bahá'í faith, and it has a large university, countless museums and a relaxed pace.

Bahá'í Shrine of the Bab and Persian Gardens

Haifa's most impressive landmark takes pride of place in the heart of the city and has become the symbol of Haifa. The perfectly manicured Persian Gardens tumble down the hill that characterises Haifa's topography and into the German Colony below, at their centre the golden-topped Bahá'í Shrine

See pp86–7 for drive route

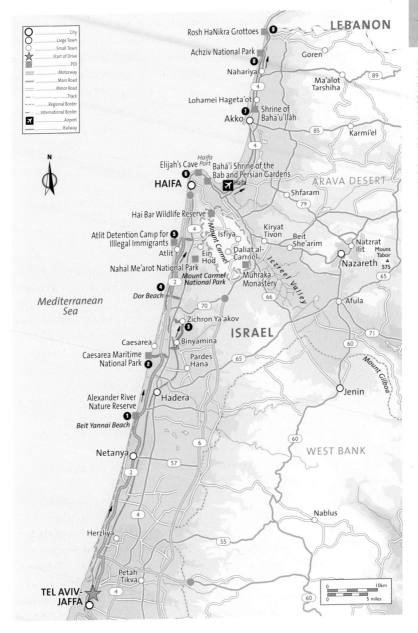

Mediterranean coast

of the Bab, named in honour of the founder of the Bahá'í faith. While it may be the most impressive of the Bahá'í shrines, it is, in fact, the second holiest – the most sacred being that of the Shrine of Bahá'u'lláh just outside Akko (*see p81*). Haifa has become the headquarters of the Bahá'í faith (*see p16*), and the shrine and Seat of the Universal House of Justice were constructed in 1943 and 1978 respectively. In 2008, the shrine and gardens were designated a UNESCO World Heritage Site. Volunteers provide free guided tours around the gardens daily except Wednesdays – these begin from the Yefe Nof Street entrance. At the time of writing the shrine was closed for renovations due to be completed in spring 2012.

Persian Gardens. Tel: (04) 831 3131.
Open: daily 9am–5pm.
Closed: 9 Jul & 2 May.
Free admission & tour.
Shrine of Bab. Open: daily 9am–12pm.
Free admission. Modest dress required.

Haifa

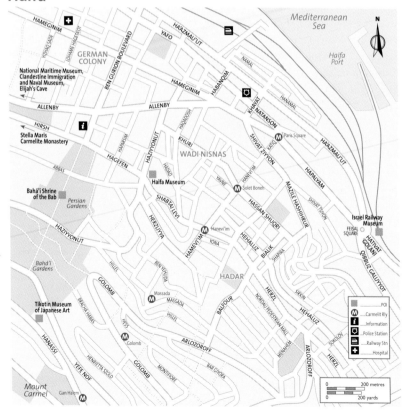

The Bahá'í Shrine and Gardens, Haifa

Elijah's Cave

At the base of Mount Carmel in the midst of bustling Haifa is Elijah's Cave, revered and worshipped by Jews, Christians, Muslims and Druze alike. It is believed to be the spot where the Hebrew prophet Elijah lived and taught and it is an important pilgrimage site for thousands of people of differing faiths every year. Until 1948, a mosque stood here, but today, a small altar is located within the cave.

230 Allenby Rd. Tel: (04) 852 7430. Open: Sun–Thur 8am–6pm, Fri 8am–1pm. Free admission. Modest dress and head coverings required; the latter are supplied at the entrance along with candles.

German Colony

Adjacent to the Bahá'í Gardens lies the area known as the German Colony, with Ben Gurion Boulevard forming the main street within this charming neighbourhood. The area was founded in 1869 by the German Templars Society, a movement created in 1861 and led by theologist Christoph Hoffman. Following harsh socio-economic conditions in Germany at the time, the society was formed with the ideals of living by the basic values of Christianity, with family and community at its core. Members believed they must gather in the Land of God and so several of these colonies appeared in the Holy Land around this time. Although there were no more than an estimated 1,700 followers in the Holy Land, their impact on agricultural techniques, urban modernisation, industry and transport was huge. The German Templars were eventually expelled by the British Mandate authorities following World War I, but their neighbourhood remains today one of Haifa's most alluring places to visit. A leafy boulevard is lined with beautiful boutique hotels, shady garden cafés, ice-cream parlours and historic buildings.

Museums
Clandestine Immigration and Naval Museum

The museum is easily recognised by the ship, the *Af Al-Pi*, resting on its roof. The ship is a tank-landing craft which brought Jewish immigrants to Palestine and broke through the British Mandate authority blockades. The museum tells the story of the hardships Jews faced attempting to immigrate, as well as the history of the Israeli navy.

204 Allenby Rd. Tel: (04) 853 6249. Open: Sun–Thur 8.30am–4pm. Admission charge.

Mount Carmel

Mount Carmel hit international headlines on 2 December 2010 when a devastating and ferocious fire broke out and started spreading rapidly across the dry vegetation. Israel's firefighting teams did their utmost to control the blaze, but eventually Prime Minister Benjamin Netanyahu sent out a plea for help. Firefighters, helicopters and water planes from the US, Turkey, Greece, the Netherlands, Switzerland, Cyprus, Russia and the UK quickly mobilised, and help from countless other countries was offered. Together they managed to extinguish the blaze, but not before 44 lives were lost and vast tracts of the once picturesque landscape were reduced to charred scrub.

Stretching 23km (14 miles) from the tip of Haifa along the Mediterranean coast, pre-fire Mount Carmel was characterised by rolling green hills, great pine forests, Druze villages and numerous historic and archaeological sites. Most of the area is encompassed by the Mount Carmel National Park, including the Hai Bar Wildlife Reserve that works towards reintroducing native species back into the wild. During the fire, despite the flames licking at the enclosures of the animals, park rangers and volunteers managed to save the roe deer and vultures which are bred here.

The area has long been home to Druze communities whose hospitality and traditional foods are known across the country. The two largest towns of Isfiya and Daliat al-Carmel are home to traditionally clad Druze elders, while in small clearings in the forests (the southern ones, which were not destroyed in the fire), families set up rudimentary stalls selling freshly pressed olive oil and home-cooked foods.

Sacred to Jews, Christians, Muslims, Druze and Bahá'í, Mount Carmel has had a long and colourful past. The site of the discovery of Neanderthal remains – in what is today the Nahal Me'arot National Park – as well as famous and significant battles throughout the centuries, the mountain has played a pivotal role in revolts, rebellions and religious struggles. According to tradition, the Prophet Elijah battled the Priests of Baal, and later the Carmelites built Muhraka Monastery to commemorate this event. Today, the monastery provides staggering views over the Jezreel Valley. During World War I,

General Allenby's victory on Mount Carmel was seen as a major turning point in the war against the Ottomans, marking yet another event in the region's tumultuous past.

Yet despite fires and battles, the Carmel is known today as one of the most peaceful and beautiful parts of the country, and while the northern portion has been destroyed for the next generation, the southern areas are as charming as ever. Ein Hod, for example, a tiny artists' village which just escaped the blaze, is the epitome of quaint, with its stone houses, cobbled lanes, appealing cafés and creative galleries, and significant archaeological sites (such as the Beit She'arim tombs) and beautiful white, sandy beaches of the Mediterranean complete the picture.

The fire did untold damage to the landscape and was the most destructive fire in Israel's history. The country was aghast at the devastation left in its wake, and deeply saddened that a region so well loved and so picturesque could be so badly marred. Yet just as the land will gradually repair itself, life in the Carmel will go on, its abundant nature, rich history and character providing plenty of opportunity for visitors to experience the charm of this region.

The Druze town of Daliat al-Carmel

Mediterranean coast

A stunning view from Mount Carmel

Haifa Museum

The museum, which also includes the Museum of Ancient Art and the Museum of Modern Art, houses archaeological finds from sites such as Caesarea, ethnographic displays of Jewish folklore, and art collections from Israeli and international artists. It is Haifa's flagship museum and certainly worth a visit.

26 Shabtai Levi St. Tel: (04) 852 3255. Open: Sun–Wed 10am–4pm, Thur 4–7pm, Fri 10am–1pm, Sat 10am–3pm. Admission charge.

Israel Railway Museum

Complete with a renovated steam train, the Ottoman station makes for an interesting setting and provides insight into the country's rail history.

1 Hativat Golani St. Tel: (04) 856 4293. Open: Sun–Thur 8.30am–3.30pm. Admission charge.

National Maritime Museum

Dedicated to 5,000 years of maritime history of the Mediterranean, Red Sea and Nile regions, the museum has varied collections and displays, including maps, models, artefacts, instruments, piracy and mythology.

198 Allenby Avenue. Tel: (04) 853 6622. Open: Sun–Thur 10am–4pm, Fri 10am–1pm, Sat 10am–3pm. Admission charge.

Tikotin Museum of Japanese Art

This unusual museum is the only one of its kind in the Middle East. It houses collections of Japanese arts, from paintings and sketches to sculpture, as well as a huge library.

89 HaNassi Avenue. Tel: (04) 838 3554. Open: Sun–Thur 10am–4pm, Fri 10am–1pm, Sat 10am–3pm. Admission charge.

Stella Maris Carmelite Monastery

Proffering spectacular views over the Mediterranean coastline, the Stella Maris is a 19th-century building constructed of smooth Italian marble. It was built by the Carmelite order, a group of religious hermits that, during the Crusader period, lived in caves in the hillside. Within a century these hermits had organised themselves into the Carmelite order, which swept across Europe. The Carmel monks were exiled during the Mamluk period but returned to build their monastery in 1836. An earlier building on this site was used as a hospital for Napoleon's injured soldiers during his campaign in the Holy Land. Inside, colourful frescoes adorn the great dome and monks will gladly pass out free leaflets.

Stella Maris. Tel: (04) 833 7758. Open: Mon–Sat 6.20am–12.30pm & 3–6pm. Free admission. Modest dress required.

Wadi Nisnas

Wadi Nisnas is a neighbourhood that has come to define peaceful coexistence, where Arabic and Jewish residents cohabit respectfully and harmoniously. Every December, the Hag HaHagim ('Festival of all Festivals') is celebrated, representing Christian Christmas, Jewish Hannukah and Muslin Ramadan. Its creation is thanks to Beit HaGefen ('House of the Vine'), an Arab–Jewish centre that promotes inter-ethnic harmony; its successful efforts are today being realised internationally. Artistic flair is also embraced, and during Hag HaHagim, outdoor galleries line the neighbourhood streets. During the rest of the year, it is highly recommended to walk the lanes of Wadi Nisnas and visit Beit HaGefen, which organises many activities, tours and programmes.

Beit HaGefen. 2 HaGefen St. Tel: (04) 852 5252. Open: Sun–Thur 8am–1pm & 4–8pm, Fri 8am–1pm, Sat 10am–1pm. Free admission.

The dome of the Stella Maris Carmelite monastery

Mediterranean coast

AKKO

Akko's Old City is one of the country's most charismatic places to visit, where a wonderful assortment of buildings, dotted by minarets and church spires and encompassed by a great citadel and imposing walls, tell the story of its complex and intriguing history. Crusaders, Mamluks, Ottomans, Napoleon, the British Mandate authorities and Jewish freedom fighters between them form a multifaceted past, while today Akko is a lively Arab city, with a bustling market, quaint fishing port and a wealth of historic interest.

Al-Basha Hammam (Municipal Museum)

Built by Al-Jazzar as part of his mosque complex, these were baths constructed in the style of Roman bathhouses. Today, they form a unique museum experience with ancient statues, lights, sounds and a tour by a holographic bath attendant.

Tel: (04) 955 1088. Open: summer Sat–Thur 8.30am–6pm, Fri 8.30am–5pm; winter Sat–Thur 8.30am–5pm, Fri 8.30am–2pm. Admission charge.

Al-Jazzar Mosque

The mosque is not only the largest in the city but the largest in the country outside Jerusalem. It was built in 1781, on the site of a Crusader church, by the Ottoman ruler Ahmed Al-Jazzar in the Turkish rococo architectural style. Inside the mosque are housed what are believed to be hairs belonging to the Prophet Muhammad and which, once a year at the end of Ramadan, are put on display to the public. Within the mosque complex are also the

Beautiful rococo decoration in the Al-Jazzar Mosque, Akko

Akko's citadel

sarcophagi of Al-Jazzar and his successor, Suleiman Pasha.
Open: Sat–Thur 8am–6pm, Fri 8–11am & 1–6pm. Admission charge. Modest dress required.

AKKO'S CITY WALLS

The bulky, pentagonal-shaped walls of Akko's Old City constitute one of its most striking features. They were originally built over the remains of Crusader structures and were later refortified by Al-Jazzar into the strong defences we see today. The walls encompass the Old City, protecting it from both land and sea assault, and played a crucial part in the defeat of Napoleon's army. Walking the walls' promenade provides views over the array of cobbled lanes, minarets and church spires as well as out to sea and is hugely recommended. To see the walls from a different angle, boat trips chug in and out of the harbour at regular intervals.

Citadel

The great citadel that today stands over the Crusader city owes its origins to the Ottoman period, when the ruler Al-Jazzar refortified the near-abandoned and crumbling city. Al-Jazzar ruled until 1804, during which time his strong citadel not only withstood attacks from Napoleon's army but also forced them to retreat. It was during this time too that the founder of the Bahá'í faith, Bahá'u'lláh, was imprisoned here, and his cell can be visited. In 1831, Ibrahim Pasha, General of Egypt, conquered the city and the citadel became his headquarters and the capital of the Galilee until 1919, during which time a large prison was built. During the British Mandate period, the citadel was converted into government buildings as well as the largest prison in the country, housing Jewish Zionist underground fighters. It lives in infamy as the scene of an attempted prison escape by members of the Irgun militant group who broke into the citadel to free the prisoners. Although foiled, it was seen as an important step for Jewish freedom fighters in terms of weakening the British control. The prison has been left untouched and today forms the Underground Prisoners Museum, a grim memorial to the nine Jewish fighters who were hanged here. The noose from which they were hanged, as well as photographs and documents, are on grisly display.

Citadel and Underground Prisoners Museum. Tel: (04) 991 8264/5/6. Open: Sun–Thur 9am–5pm, Fri 9am–1pm. Admission charge.

Khans

Several large khans can be found in the old city, the largest and most impressive being Khan El-Umdan. These khans were in fact merchants' inns built around a large central courtyard, and acted as a hotel and storerooms for the numbers of merchants arriving into Akko's thriving port during the 16th, 17th and 18th centuries. At the time of writing, Khan El-Umdan was closed to the public for renovations, but it is usually a worthwhile and interesting place to explore. The oldest dated khan is Khan El-Faranj, built by French merchants. Only the courtyard is open to the public.

Market street

Running through the heart of the Old City is this lively, colourful and fascinating bazaar. Shoe-horned into the cobbled lanes, it weaves its way through the churches, mosques and khans and is a flurry of noise and activity. The multifarious stalls sell traditional Arab fare such as sweet sticky baklava, fresh fruit juices, dried fruit, nuts, spices, hummus and olives, as well as fresh meats, baked goods, household items and glass *narghile* pipes.
Open: daily until 5pm.

Wares for sale in Akko's colourful bazaar

81

Mediterranean coast

Shrine of Bahá'u'lláh

Located just outside Akko is the Shrine of Bahá'u'lláh, founder of the Bahá'í faith. It is the holiest site for the Bahá'í (the second holiest being the Shrine of the Bab in Haifa, *see pp70 & 72*) and the focus of pilgrimage for followers from around the world. After his release from Akko prison, Bahá'u'lláh spent his final days in the beautiful Mansion of Bahji and was buried in the adjacent shrine. Perfectly manicured gardens offer an air of peaceful tranquillity and there are daily tours (except on Wednesdays) around the site.
Bustan HaGalil. Tel: (04) 831 3131. Gardens open: 9am–5pm daily. Shrine open: Sun–Fri 9am–noon. Free admission. Modest dress required. Bus: 271 (stops at Bustan HaGalil for access to north gate).

Underground Crusader City

Akko was a crucial port city for hundreds of years, and when the Crusaders invaded Palestine, the Knights Hospitaller made it their capital in the Holy Land. Here, they built a huge fortress, which they abandoned following their defeat and which lay forgotten, eventually becoming hidden beneath the great citadel that was built over it. Extensive excavations that began in 1950 and continue to this day have so far revealed a series of huge Gothic rooms with high, vaulted ceilings, big windows and ornate columns. The most impressive rooms are the halls, one of which served as a conference and ceremonial hall for the knights of the order, the other as a dining room. Other rooms include a dormitory, storerooms, reservoirs and toilets.
Tel: (04) 995 6706. Open: Sun–Thur & Sat 8.30am–6pm, Fri 8.30am–5pm. Admission charge.

ZICHRON YA'AKOV

Located on the southern end of Mount Carmel, on a rise above the Mediterranean coast, Zichron Ya'akov is about as bucolic as it gets. Quiet, leafy roads surround a central, pedestrian-only cobbled street lined with artists' workshops, patio cafés and historic buildings. The town is small yet significant as an early Zionist settlement, the final resting place of Baron Edmond de Rothschild, and the site of one of the country's premier wineries.

The Wine Road

The Wine Road is in fact HaMeyasdim Street, running through the centre of the town. It underwent a huge renovation project to bring it back to its former glory as one of Rothschild's colonies during the First Aliyah (Jewish immigration). The houses' façades were restored and characteristic features reintroduced, including wooden window frames, tiled roofs, wood fences and street lamps. The street begins at the cemetery and ends at the winery at the other end of town. In addition to the places listed below, the Ohel Ya'akov Synagogue, which was built by Rothschild in 1882, is also located on the Wine Road. It was considered the

The renovated Wine Road, Zichron Ya'akov

somewhat of a martyr for her refusal to divulge information following her capture by the Turks, and her subsequent suicide.
40 HaMeyasdim St. Open: Sun, Mon, Wed & Thur 8.30am–3pm, Tue 8.30am–5pm, Fri 8.30am–1pm. Admission charge.

Carmel Winery

In 1882, Baron Edmond de Rothschild started the Carmel Winery and to this day it remains the biggest and most successful in Israel. The Carmel Winery in fact owns 1,400 hectares (3,460 acres) of land throughout the country, which allows its vines to be chosen from different soils and geographical zones. It sells 15 million bottles a year, ranging from the Carmel Limited Edition, the flagship of the winery, to Selected, Israel's best-selling brand, and all Carmel wines are kosher.

The Center for Carmel Wine & Culture located in Zichron Ya'akov has a wine shop, restaurant, two tasting rooms, a small movie room and a barrel room located in one of Rothschild's original cellars. Visitors can experience the winemaking process as well as learn about the history of Israel's oldest winery.
Tel: (04) 639 1788. www.carmelwines.co.il

Cemetery

With views over the Mediterranean Sea and shaded by trees, Zichron Ya'akov's cemetery is a peaceful and beautiful

grandest and most beautiful synagogue in the country at the time. Another sight worth visiting is the Water Tower, which also dates from the First Aliyah and offers excellent views from the top.

Aaronson House

The house acts as a memorial and museum in honour of Aaron Aaronson and his sister, Sarah. Aaron was a well-respected botanist who created the Nili group, a spy ring that divulged Turkish secrets to the British during World War I, and both he and Sarah were at the centre of this ring. From their home in Zichron Ya'akov they spent years working underground, and the museum now holds papers, photographs and documents relating to their espionage. Both are regarded as Jewish heroes, and Sarah is heralded as place – so much so that Baron Rothschild expressed his wish to be buried there upon his death. In 1954, 19 years after he died, the bodies of both he and his wife were transported aboard a naval ship from his home country of France to Israel, where he received a state funeral. His mausoleum is located in the centre of the cemetery – which is within a nature reserve – and a stone-carved map of the country shows the extent of the lands he purchased and the colonies he established.

First Aliyah Museum

When influxes of Jews arrived in Palestine between 1882 and 1904, Zichron Ya'akov was one of the most sought-after places in which to settle, and the museum tells the story of these early arrivals. It is housed in the town

EDMOND DE ROTHSCHILD

Born into the prestigious and hugely wealthy French banking family, Edmond's interests lay less in banking and more in the arts and sciences. He founded countless scientific institutions throughout Europe and owned a priceless collection of art, yet from 1882 he began spending less money on the arts and more on purchasing large tracts of land in Palestine, spending in excess of 50 million dollars and acquiring more than 50,600 hectares (125,000 acres) of land. As one of the foremost advocates of the Zionist movement, Rothschild wanted a safe place for Jews in the Holy Land, but famously stated that 'the struggle to put an end to the Wandering Jew could not have as its result the creation of the Wandering Arab'.

hall built by Rothschild over 100 years ago – at the time considered one of the most impressive buildings in the country – and, among its many artefacts and photographs, contains a short black-and-white video believed to be the oldest film of the country.
2 HaNadiv St. Tel: (04) 629 4777. Open: Mon & Wed–Fri 9am–2pm, Tue 9am–3pm. Admission charge.

CAESAREA

It seems the town of Caesarea has always been an affluent area. Today, mansions line wide streets of the new town, yet Caesarea is one of the country's top tourist destinations not for its plush houses but for the vast archaeological site sitting on the Mediterranean shore. The site played a crucial role in the Byzantine period when great churches were built, and

Aaronson House, Zichron Ya'akov

before that during Roman rule under Herod, when it was named after the Roman Emperor Caesar. Caesarea became one of the biggest and most important port cities in the world and was the site of the declaration of Vespasian as Emperor of the Roman Empire, the trial of Paul the Apostle and the home of Pontius Pilate. The later Crusader city became a heavily fortified stronghold in the Holy Land and many of its stout defences date from this time. The sights listed below are located within the Caesarea Maritime National Park (*Tel: (04) 626 7080. www.caesarea.com. Open: Sun–Thur 8am–6pm, Fri 8am–4pm; closes one hour earlier in winter. Admission charge*).

Aqueduct

The aqueduct was a crucial feature of Herod's city, bringing in fresh water to the residents. The Roman aqueduct begins some 15km (9 miles) north of Caesarea at the foot of Mount Carmel and is a fine example of architectural and engineering prowess. The aqueduct was later extended by Hadrian and then the Crusaders and can be seen in parts as you drive along the main road south towards the archaeological site.

Bathhouses

In Roman times, the city's bathhouses were an important social focal point, where the higher echelons of society would come to discuss affairs. Today, the excavated remains of the 4th-

CRUSADER CITY

With battles raging between the Crusaders and the Arabs, Caesarea found itself heavily fortified under Crusader rule. A 4m (13ft)-thick wall was built around the city running for 1.6km (1 mile), as well as towers and a moat. Today, access to the Crusader city is through the sturdy and imposing East Gate and, once inside, the remains of the Temple of Augustus and the cathedral can be seen. The old harbour in its present form also dates from the Crusaders' time, and columns can be seen protruding from the harbour wall.

century structure are an excellent example of Roman architecture, and the distinct rooms that made up the complex are visible along with their ornate mosaics.

Byzantine street

These are the remains of a Byzantine street of shops. Steps lead up to what was the forecourt with a mosaic floor, and just inside this are the remains of two headless statues. One is made from white marble and the other a purple stone known as porphyry, the use of which was generally restricted to rendering imperial images. The porphyry is likely to have been a statue of Emperor Hadrian, who rebuilt much of the Herodian city after natural disasters destroyed the harbour and parts of the city.

Herod's Roman theatre

Probably the most impressive feature at Caesarea is the fully restored theatre built by Herod in 22–10 BC, with an impressive seating capacity of 4,000 people. With a backdrop of crashing Mediterranean waves, it is an idyllic setting, and today concerts are held here in summer. The vast semicircular theatre was built of granite columns from Aswan, Egypt, and contained a significant inscription that mentioned the Roman governor, Pontius Pilate, who lived in Caesarea and was a key figure in the trial of Jesus. Today, the original inscription is in the Israel Museum in Jerusalem and a replica has replaced it.

Hippodrome

The massive hippodrome (230m by 80m/755ft by 262ft) would have been the centre of Roman entertainment, where great chariot races entertained the 20,000 spectators that it could accommodate. Today, the hippodrome takes centre stage within the archaeological park and gives visitors a true glimpse of the extent of this vast city.

Promontory palace

Located on a stretch of land jutting out into the sea is the site of King Herod's lavish palace. Measuring 110m by 60m (360ft by 197ft), the palace was designed in extravagance with mosaic floors, a large central pool and ornate porticos. The palace was located in the southern portion of the Roman city and is easily recognised by remains of marble columns.

Underwater Archeological Park

Herod's great port today lies underneath several metres of water and has become a hugely interesting and unique marine archaeological site. Scuba divers can either follow a guide or guide themselves, with the help of numbered markers and a map, around the great harbour walls and ancient anchors.
Tel: (04) 626 5898. www.caesarea-diving.com. Admission charge.

The extensive Roman ruins at Caesarea

Drive: The Mediterranean coast

Following the coastal road north from Tel Aviv to the border with Lebanon affords a wonderful glimpse of a cross-section of Israeli life and provides a chance to get out of the main towns and explore significant archaeological sites, pretty villages, wild beaches and nature reserves.

The route (see map on p71) covers 150km (93 miles) and takes around two hours to drive.

Start in Tel Aviv and head north on Route 2 for 42km (26 miles) to reach Beit Yannai Beach.

1 Beit Yannai Beach and the Alexander River

Just north of Netanya is this wild sweep of beach. Kite-surfers whip across the waves and youngsters from surrounding villages barbecue and frolic on the sand. A little north is the Alexander River Nature Reserve, home to endangered green turtles.

Continue north on Route 2 for 18km (11 miles) to Caesarea.

2 Caesarea

Up there with the world's great archaeological sites is Herod's Roman port city, with its impressive theatre, hippodrome and underwater national park (*see pp83–5*).

Head inland on Route 6511 and at the roundabout go north on Route 4. Continue heading north for 8km (5 miles) and then follow signs up Nili Road (right) to Zichron Ya'akov.

3 Zichron Ya'akov

This irrepressibly quaint town is famed as the premier colony of Zionist Baron Rothschild, as well as his final resting place and home to the country's largest winery (*see pp81–3*).

Head north on Route 4, cross Foradis Junction and approximately 3km (2 miles) further on, turn left to Dor.

4 Dor Beach

Possibly the prettiest Mediterranean beach, it has three sheltered bays carved out of the rocks to form natural, shallow pools of turquoise water and white sand.

Head back on to Route 4 and continue north for 12km (7½ miles) to Atlit.

5 Atlit Detention Camp for Illegal Immigrants

Just outside Atlit village are the remains of a detention camp set up by the British to house Jewish immigrants

The Tel Aviv coastline

arriving in Palestine. The site commemorates the immigrants, many escaping persecution from both the Nazi regime and Arab countries, and depicts individual stories. Leaving the site, look out for an old ship on the side of the motorway which was one of 130 vessels used to transport the refugees.
Head north on Route 2 to Haifa.

6 Haifa
Check out the Bahá'í Shrine, plus some excellent museums and beaches (*see pp70–77*).
Continue 25km (15 miles) north on Route 4 to Akko, and turn left at the signpost to Akko Old City.

7 Akko
Cobbled lanes, minarets, the imposing citadel, Crusader remains, a bustling bazaar and busy fishing port are undoubted highlights here (*see pp78–81*).
Head north on Route 4 for 15km (9 miles) to the Achziv turn-off.

8 Achziv National Park
A rocky coast leads down to wide sandy beaches that attract nesting sea turtles by night and sun-seekers by day. Deep, sheltered pools have formed along the coast and amid the lawns are the remains of an ancient town.
3km (2 miles) north on Route 4, you will find the Rosh HaNikra Grottoes.

9 Rosh HaNikra Grottoes
Straddling the border with Lebanon are large, chalk grottoes, carved out of the cliff over hundreds of years. A cable car leads down to the caves, where penetrating sunlight creates turquoise pools. Tunnels that lead through the cliff into present-day Lebanon have been used by people for centuries, including Alexander the Great and Jews fleeing Nazi Europe and the 1948 Arab–Israeli War.
To return to Tel Aviv, head south, back along Route 4 the whole way.

Drive: The Mediterranean coast

Galilee

Forming the northern lands of Israel, the Galilee (HaGalil in Hebrew) is steeped in rural charm. Green rolling hills, forested valleys, flowing streams and at its centre the Sea of Galilee (Kinneret in Hebrew) make it one of the prettiest regions in the country. Significant historical events were played out on these soils at sites such as Tel Megiddo, a crucial stop for the north–south trade caravans that once swept through the valley from Damascus.

On the shores of the glittering Sea of Galilee, small churches, green fields and villages see scores of pilgrims coming to walk in the footsteps of Jesus who performed many of his miracles around the lake, while the party town of Tiberias is one of the four holy Jewish cities. Tzfat is another of the holy cities and sits snuggled among the pine trees of the Upper Galilee, adorned with cobbled lanes and ancient synagogues exuding religious observance and an air of mysticism, while nearby, the picturesque town of Rosh Pina is a flourishing artists' colony. The charming and beautiful hilltop city of Nazareth is both a busy Arab enclave and traditionally known to be the childhood home of Jesus, while the Jezreel Valley below is home to fields of wild flowers, prime agricultural land, great archaeological sites and picturesque national parks. In the northern stretches of the region, the Jordan River makes for a top rafting destination, the Hula Valley is one of the world's best birdwatching spots, and other lovely valleys and forests blanket the countryside.

NAZARETH

Known as Jesus' childhood home and the scene of Mary's annunciation, Nazareth attracts huge numbers of pilgrims from across the world. The predominantly Arab-Christian city has at its heart the Old City, where tiny, cobbled lanes weave haphazardly between churches, mosques and a busy souk. Modest dress is required throughout the city, but especially so when entering religious buildings.

Basilica of the Annunciation

The towering Catholic church that takes pride of place in the centre of the city was built over earlier Byzantine and Crusader ones, the site having long been a place of pilgrimage. Within the vast church complex is the Grotto of the Annunciation, believed in Catholic tradition to be the site where the Virgin

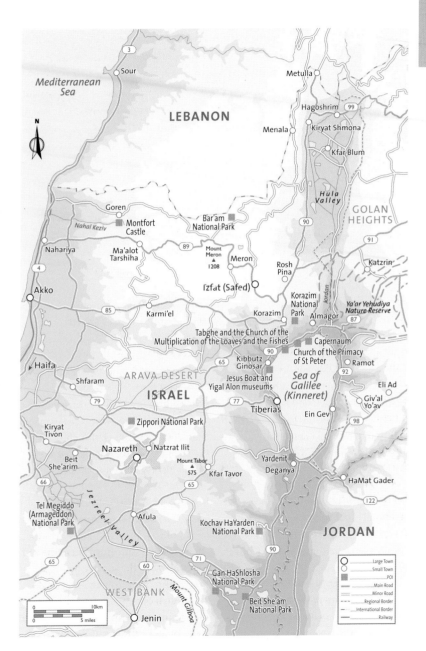

Mediterranean
Sea

Sour

Metulla

Hagoshrim 99

LEBANON

Menala

Kiryat Shmona

Kfar Blum

Hula
Valley

GOLAN
HEIGHTS

Goren

Montfort
Castle

Bar'am
National Park

90

Nahal Keziv

91

Nahariya

Ma'alot
Tarshiha

89

Mount
Meron
1208

Meron

Rosh
Pina

Katzrin

Izfat (Safed)

Akko

85

Karmi'el

Korazim

Korazim
National
Park

Almagor

Ya'ar Yehudiya
Nature Reserve

87

Tabghe and the Church of the
Multiplication of the Loaves and the Fishes

90

Capernaum

Church of the Primacy
of St Peter

Haifa

ARAVA DESERT

65

Kibbutz
Ginosar

Ramot

92

Shfaram

ISRAEL

79

Jesus Boat and
Yigal Alon museums

77

Sea of
Galilee
(Kinneret)

Eli Ad

Giv'al
Yo'av

Tiberias

Ein Gev

98

Kiryat
Tivon

Zippori National Park

Beit
She'arim

Nazareth

Natzrat Ilit

66

Mount Tabor
575

Kfar Tavor

Yardenit

Deganya

HaMat Gader

Tel Megiddo
(Armageddon)
National Park

65

Afula

Kochav HaYarden
National Park

JORDAN

122

Jezreel Valley

90

○ ....Large Town
○ ....Small Town
■ ....POI
___ ....Main Road
___ ....Minor Road
-·-·- ....Regional Border
-·-·- ....International Border
___ ....Railway

65

60

71

Gan HaShlosha
National Park

WEST BANK

Mount Gilboa

Beit She'an
National Park

0   10km

0   5 miles

Jenin

Basilica of the Annunciation, Nazareth

Mary received the news from the Archangel Gabriel of her impending motherhood. The church is fortress-like, standing 55m (180ft) high with strong, high walls and a concrete dome. Yet it is strangely beautiful, with a mixture of modern ecclesiastical designs and the remains of the old churches visible from the grotto. The upper church is decorated with mosaics from Catholic communities around the world.
Casanova St. Open: Mon–Sat 8am–6pm, Sun & public holidays 2–5.30pm. Free admission. Modest dress required.

Greek Catholic Synagogue Church

This small site is believed to be the synagogue where Jesus studied and prayed and where he preached to the people of Nazareth. Early on it became an important site of pilgrimage, leading to the construction of a small church which today is Greek Catholic. Underneath the church is a synagogue, and while tradition has it that this was the very one where Jesus delivered his sermon, it most likely dates from the 6th century. To find the synagogue church, turn left at the top of the main market street and then take the first right. There is a small stone entrance on the right that is easily missed.
*Old City. Tel: (04) 656 8488.
Open: Mon–Sat 8am–noon & 2–5pm. Free admission. Modest dress required.*

Mary's Well and the Church of St Gabriel

The Orthodox contender for the site where Gabriel visited Mary is the spring which emerges under today's Church of St Gabriel. As tradition has it, Mary was collecting water from a well when the Archangel Gabriel came and gave her the news of Jesus' birth. The well in the square located at the top of Paulus VI Street is modern, but the spring is believed to be ancient. Indeed, investigations under a nearby souvenir shop uncovered an ancient Roman bathhouse which would have been present during Jesus' time. A small aisle leads through the Church of St Gabriel to an altar over which it is possible to look down on to the spring below. *Casanova St. Open: Mon–Sat 8am–5pm, Sun noon–2pm. Free admission. Modest dress required.*

Nazareth souk

Snaking its way through the narrow streets of the Old City is the Nazareth souk, one of the largest markets in the country. Despite the foreign visitors that wander past the stalls, the market is an authentic Arab shopping area, frequented by people from Nazareth and beyond. Narrow shops spill their wares into the lanes outside, selling a selection of clothes, household items, spices and fresh foods. It's easy to lose yourself here – and certainly the best way to fully experience its charm. The market begins at the top of Casanova Street just off the central Paulus V Street that traverses the city centre.

Nazareth Village

A full reconstruction of Nazareth as it would likely have appeared in Jesus' time has been built with meticulous attention to detail and has become a popular tourist attraction, especially for families. Agricultural techniques, food

Mary's Well and the Church of St Gabriel

presses, traditional costumes and food are displayed or demonstrated, and sheep and other animals wander around the grounds.
Old City. Tel: (04) 645 6042. www.nazarethvillage.com. Open: Mon–Sat 9am–5pm. Admission charge.

St Joseph's Church
The Franciscan church that stands today was built on the traditional site of Joseph's carpentry workshop over earlier churches commemorating Joseph. Within the church are an ancient water pit, mosaics, caves and barns from ancient Nazareth dating from the 1st and 2nd centuries BC. It is one of these caves that is believed to have been Joseph's workshop and so marks another point on the pilgrimage trail. The church is located 50m (55yds) from the northern exit of the Basilica of the Annunication.
Old City. Tel: (04) 657 2501. Open: daily 7am–6pm. Free admission. Modest dress required.

The White Mosque (Al-Abiad)
The mosque is located in the heart of the Old City and owes its origins to the times of the Akko governor Al-Jazzar – and more importantly commemorates the end of his iron-fisted rule in the early 19th century. The slender style and white colour was chosen to represent purity, simplicity and the peaceful coexistence of the different religions in Nazareth. In fact, the mosque stands as a lovely example of

religious tolerance, and it sends out a message of peace and harmony to the people of the city and to other religious denominations.
Old City. Tel: (04) 656 9061. Open: daily, except during prayer times. Free admission. Modest dress required.

JEZREEL VALLEY
Sweeping across the Galilee, the Jezreel Valley is a splash of fertile green fields, small kibbutzim and village communities, and staggering archaeological sites. It stretches from Mount Carmel in the west to the Sea of Galilee and Jordan River in the east and has been an important agricultural area for centuries.

Beit She'an National Park
The outstanding archaeological remains of Beit She'an come as a surprise to many as they drive through the nondescript town in which they lie. The magnitude of the remains is breathtaking, the entire Roman city having been destroyed in one moment during a devastating earthquake in AD 749. An excavated single upright column is a poignant reminder of the instant destruction of a once-prosperous city. Set in a critical position amid fertile lands along the Via Maris trade highway, the city was inhabited for 4,500 years. Yet its most impressive remains date from the glorious days of its Roman occupation, when it became one of the ten cities that formed the Decapolis. The

amphitheatre, bathhouses and fountains are its most impressive relics but the site as a whole is hugely atmospheric. The new She'an Nights is a light show played out on the hill to the north of the site and depicts the history of Beit She'an (*shows run Mon, Wed, Thur & Sat every half hour after sunset. Admission charge*).
Beit She'an National Park. Tel: (04) 658 7189. www.parks.org.il. Open: Sun–Thur 8am–5pm, Fri 8am–4pm, Sat 8am–5pm; closes one hour earlier in winter. Admission charge. Buses 948, 961 & 966 (Tiberias–Jerusalem) & 829 & 843 (Tel Aviv–Beit She'an) all stop in Beit She'an.

Gan HaShlosha National Park

Crystal-clear spring water erupts into a series of pools surrounded by green lawns at one of the country's prettiest national parks. Outside school holidays, when the vast crowds are absent, the park makes for a tranquil day of swimming, lounging under waterfalls and having a barbecue beneath the trees.
Tel: (04) 658 6219. www.parks.org.il. Open: Apr–Sept 8am–5pm; Oct–Mar 8am–4pm. Admission charge. Buses 411 & 412 (Beit She'an–Afula) stop outside.

Kochav HaYarden National Park

An impressive, heavily moated Crusader castle, Belvoir Castle, sits atop the high ridge, from where panoramic views of the Galilee would have provided it with a crucial strategic vantage point. It is one of the best-preserved castles in the country. Also of interest in the national park is a sanctuary for Egyptian vultures, which have called this ridge home for years. Birds crippled through the poisoning of calf carcasses by local farmers are rehabilitated and, where possible, released back into the wild.
Yissahar Ridge, 15km (9⅓ miles) north of Beit She'an. Tel: (04) 658 1766. www.parks.org.il. Open: Sat–Thur 8am–5pm, Fri 8am–4pm; closes one hour earlier in winter. Admission charge. Bus 28 (Tiberias–Beit She'an) will drop you on the main road, necessitating a 6km (3¾-mile) uphill walk to the entrance.

Mount Tabor

The round, 575m (1,886ft)-high hill is an easily recognisable landmark in the

Mount Tabor and the Jezreel Valley

Jezreel landscape, and one that sees scores of pilgrims ascend to its summit to visit the Catholic Church of the Transfiguration. This is believed to be the site upon which Jesus was accepted as the Son of God, although there are several other contenders for this elsewhere in the country. In Jewish tradition, this was the site of the battle in which Deborah and Barak defeated Sisera. Cars and buses are no longer allowed up the hill so visitors must ascend the stone steps on foot.

The lower slopes are home to several small Arab communities, where stalls selling traditional, home-cooked food can be found, and the area is a popular one with cyclists and hikers.
Church of the Transfiguration.
Open: Sun–Fri 8am–noon & 2–5pm.
Free admission. Modest dress required.

Tel Megiddo (Armageddon)

On a tel (man-made hill) overlooking the valley is the site of Tel Megiddo, also known as Armageddon. Christian tradition predicts that this will be the site of the end of the world, and considering its tumultuous past, it is perhaps a fair assumption! Twenty-six phases of occupation have been discovered here, dating from 4000 BC to 400 BC, one built over another. Its crucial location was its raison d'être and why it was such a sought-after piece of land. It falls on two major crossroads, and controlling Megiddo meant controlling the great trade caravans that swept down from

Damascus towards Egypt along the Via Maris trade highway. Today, the most impressive remains date from the reign of King Solomon, who built a great fortress and vast city here. The excavations of Solomon's stables and the fortress are visible, and an ancient water system can be explored.
Tel: (04) 659 0316. www.parks.org.il.
Open: Sat–Thur 8am–5pm, Fri 8am–
4pm. Admission charge. Buses 823
(Tel Aviv–Nazareth) & 841, 830 & 835
(Tel Aviv–Tiberias) will drop you at
the Megiddo Junction, leaving a 2km
(1¼-mile) walk to the entrance.

Zippori National Park

Located on a hill in the middle of the valley, Zippori was once a prosperous city. It was founded during the Hellenistic period and following the

The impressive remains at Zippori

Roman conquest was named capital of the Galilee. It is famed as being one of the few cities that did not join the revolt against the Romans in AD 66, thus its residents escaped persecution. By the 2nd century AD, Zippori had become a centre of Judaism, and the Sanhedrin (Jewish religious and judicial body) was located here at the beginning of the 3rd century. Ornate mosaics and a Roman temple are some of the most impressive remains at the site today, and it is worth taking a guided tour to help put the complex archaeology into its historical context.

Tel: (04) 656 8272. www.parks.org.il. Open: Sat–Thur 8am–5pm, Fri 8am–4pm. Admission charge. Bus 343 (from Nazareth & Akko) will drop you at the Zippori Junction, 4km (2½ miles) from the entrance.

Sea of Galilee

SEA OF GALILEE (KINNERET)
Beaches
The sea's beaches have been embroiled in controversy for many years over illegal privatisation and hefty entrance fees. Now a flat rate for vehicles entering the beach's car parks is charged, and there is free entry for pedestrians. The result, however, is a lack of facilities, most significantly lifeguards, meaning swimming is now prohibited at almost all the beaches.

This hasn't diminished their popularity, however, and in the summer months, Israeli teenagers set up camp for weekends of fun, loud music and barbecues. Amnon Beach, on the northern shore, is quieter and has good facilities since it is one of the few private beaches left. Likewise, the beaches of Duga and Gofra are more family-oriented, and all have campsites. Levanon (Lavnun) and Halukim beaches are known as some of the popular younger hangouts, but during school time they are much quieter and have good camping facilities. Just north of these is the wild strip of sand dunes popular with kite-surfers and known as Ashalim Beach. This is a lovely spot for daytime picnics and photographing the lake. Probably the prettiest beach is that of Ein Gev, belonging to the holiday resort village.

Buses 15 & 19 stop at Ein Gev & Levanon but there is no public transport to the other beaches.

Mount of Beatitudes Church

Churches

Across the north shore of the Sea of Galilee several churches commemorate major events in the life of Jesus and are not only some of the most important pilgrimage sites in the country, but also beautiful and serene places to visit, offering unspoilt views of the lake. These include the Church of the Primacy of St Peter, the Church of the Multiplication of the Loaves and the Fishes, the Mount of Beatitudes, and Capernaum. (*For more detailed information, see pp98–9.*)

Jesus Boat and Yigal Alon museums

The museums, which are housed within one complex and often referred to collectively as the Galilee Museum at Ginosar, has as its centrepiece the remains of an ancient wooden boat dating from the 1st century, around the time of Jesus (hence the name). It was excavated from the shores of the Sea of Galilee near Capernaum and its finding, excavation and preservation are depicted in an audiovisual presentation. Other sections of the museum are dedicated to exhibitions on Galilean culture and history, and to the life of Yigal Alon, former deputy prime minister and founder of the nearby Kibbutz Ginosar.

Kibbutz Ginosar. Tel: (04) 672 7700. www.jesusboatmuseum.com. Open: Sun–Thur 8am–5pm, Fri 8am–2pm, Sat 8am–4pm. Admission charge. Buses 59, 63, 450, 841 & 963 from Tiberias stop at the Ginosar Junction.

Korazim National Park

The impressive ruins at Korazim date from the Byzantine period, but it was during Talmudic times that it was mentioned in several sources, and then later as one of the three cities (along with Bethsaida and Capernaum) that were condemned by Jesus for not heeding his preaching. The remains of residential buildings, streets, ritual baths and olive presses are impressive, but the most magnificent are the remains of an ancient synagogue dating from the late 4th or early 5th century, intricately carved with floral, geometric and animal motifs.

Tel: (04) 693 4982. www.parks.org.il. Open: 8am–5pm. Admission charge. Buses 841 & 963 from Tiberias stop at the Korazim Junction, 2km (1¼ miles) from the entrance.

Tiberias

Historically, Tiberias was one of four holy Jewish cities (along with Jerusalem, Hebron and Tzfat) and was the seat of the Sanhedrin and centre of Jewish learning after the destruction of the Second Temple. Today, however, Tiberias does not number among the most charming cities in the country, although it has certainly improved in recent years. Popular with holidaying Israeli teenagers, it is somewhat raucous in summertime, with busy watersports centres and bars lining the Midrahov (promenade).

There are still some worthwhile sites, however, and some excellent hotels and restaurants. Scattered in the hills are the tombs of great Jewish scholars such as rabbis Maimonides, Yohanan Ben Zakkai and Ben Akiva, while the Tiberias hot springs and Hamat Tiberias National Park opposite protect and use the natural springs that have flowed here for centuries and offer therapeutic treatments and spas. The Galilee Experience is also worth a visit for its entertaining film spanning 4,000 years of Galilean history.
Bus: 961, 962 & 963 (Tiberias–Jerusalem), 830, 835 & 841 (Tiberias–Tel Aviv), 430 (Tiberias–Haifa) & 450 (Tiberias–Tzfat).

Yardenit

Located on the south of the Sea of Galilee, where the Jordan River begins its way south, is the traditional site of Jesus' baptism by John the Baptist. The emerald-coloured waters are laden with fish, and eucalyptus trees decorate the banks of the river, but for many of the visitors who come, it is the chance to be baptised in these waters that is the important part of any pilgrimage. Indeed, it is an impressive sight to see hundreds of white-robed Christians line up to descend into the Jordan River for their baptism. Call or email in advance for baptism dates and times.
Tel: (04) 675 9111. Email: yardenit@ kinneret.org.il. www.yardenit.com. Open: Sat–Thur 8am–6pm, Fri 8am– 4pm; closes one hour earlier in winter. Free admission. Buses 15 & 19 (Tiberias– Golan Heights) stop at the Ohalo Junction for Yardenit.

A baptism in the Jordan River

Walk: In Jesus' footsteps

The Sea of Galilee played a critical role in the life of Jesus, and several major biblical events happened on these shores. This walk encompasses significant biblical sites and churches built to commemorate Jesus' miracles, and makes for a hugely rewarding exploration along the least developed section of the lake, which appears today as it did hundreds of years ago.

Allow two hours to cover the 4km (2½ miles) of this walk.

Start at the northwest corner of the Sea of Galilee in the tiny lakeside hamlet of Tabghe.

1 Tabghe and the Church of the Multiplication of the Loaves and the Fishes

Tabghe is home to the church so named to commemorate Jesus' miracle of the feeding of the five thousand. It is also, according to tradition, where Jesus appeared to his disciples after his resurrection. The site is a tranquil, pretty place of reflection and worship, and the church's intricate Byzantine mosaic depicting the multiplication is particularly interesting.

Continue eastwards along the sea until you reach the Church of the Primacy of St Peter.

2 Church of the Primacy of St Peter

Here, swallows fly in and out of the small Franciscan church that rests on the beach, and it is here too that Jesus is said to have appeared to his disciples for the third time and confirmed the Apostle Peter. It is built upon a flat rock believed by Byzantine pilgrims to be the site of the *Mensa Christi* ('table of Christ', on which Jesus served food to his disciples, telling them to 'feed my sheep').

About 1km (²⁄₃ mile) further along the coast a marked path leads up from the shore to a rise known as Mount Eremos.

3 Mount of Beatitudes

The Mount of Beatitudes (Mount Eremos), is the traditional site of Jesus' Sermon on the Mount. Today, an octagonal-shaped church stands amid serene gardens, and an air of tranquillity permeates. Inside the church hangs the cloak of Pope Paul VI, a memento of his visit to Israel in 1964. Interestingly, this church was originally funded by Benito Mussolini, whose name plaque once stood in the doorway but has long been removed.

Back on the shore and heading east again you will come across the Korazim National Park, which in fact spans the whole stretch of coast from Tabghe. The land here is undeveloped and offers a true Sea of Galilee experience, with serene views over the sea and a picturesque landscape behind. The first site you will come to is the archaeological site of Capernaum.

4 Capernaum

This is famed as being the home of Jesus after he left Nazareth, and it was during his years living here that he conducted many of the miracles recorded in the Bible. It is also said to be the birthplace of St Peter, and a church, built over an earlier Byzantine one, stands above remains believed to be his house (visible from inside the church). The synagogue at Capernaum, dating from around the 3rd century, is impressive in its remains, with white marble columns showing the opulence it once had. Some believe that this is the synagogue where Jesus taught and cast out demons. A little further on from Capernaum is the attractive, red-domed Greek Orthodox Church of the Seven Apostles. The national park headquarters mark the final stop on the walk and a viewing platform here offers scenic views across the water. *To return to Tabghe, either retrace your steps or walk along the main road.*

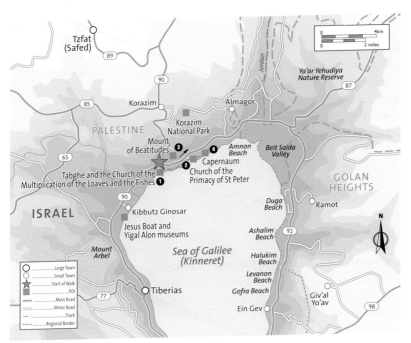

TZFAT

Tzfat (or Safed) is known as the Mystical City. One of Judaism's four holy cities, it is a centre of learning for devout Jews, in particular Kabbalah followers. The Old City is irrepressibly charming, with cobbled lanes, ancient synagogues and a flourishing Artist Colony. Traditionally clothed Orthodox Jews wander the little lanes and an old-worldly feel is palpable. Just outside the city is Mount Canaan, with its pine forest and panoramic views of the Galilee.

Artist Colony

Established in 1949 in the previously Arab part of the town, this area is a flourishing and integral part of Tzfat's cultural heritage. Over 60 galleries, workshops and exhibition halls – including the General Exhibition – dot the cobbled lanes, offering paintings, ceramics, photography and sculpture, with Kabbalah and Jewish themes dominating.

General Exhibition. HaMaayan Square. Tel: (04) 692 0087. www.artistcolony.co.il. Open: Sun– Thur 10am–6pm, Fri & Sat 10am– 2pm. Free admission.

Beit HaMeiri Museum

This family-run dairy was the country's first and today offers guided tours around the charming stone building.

Tzfat's Artist Colony

Cheese-making techniques and a tasting are included in the tour.
Keren HaYessod St. www.hameiri-cheese.co.il. Guided tours: Fri noon. Admission charge.

Crusader castle

As a crucial thoroughfare on the route to Damascus, Tzfat was fortified in 1140 when a Crusader castle was built at the top of the hill in the centre of the city. There are amazing views of Mount Canaan and the surrounding northern Galilee landscape from the top.
Free admission.

Memorial Museum of Hungarian Speaking Jewry

The small but unique museum is dedicated to the lost communities of the Hungarian Jews and is filled with displays of cultural items and memorabilia. Indeed, it is considered so valuable a collection that the Hungarian prime minister asked to see the museum on an official visit to Israel.
HaAtzmaut Square. Tel: (04) 692 3880/1. www.hjm.org.il. Open: Sun–Fri 9am–1pm. Free admission.

Old cemetery

The ancient cemetery in Tzfat is the final resting place of countless great scholars of Judaism's past. Rabbis Isaac Luria (*see 'Ashkenazi Ari Synagogue' p103*), Josef Caro (*see 'Yosef Caro Synagogue' p103*), Abuhav and Beirav are among many Jewish scholars to

have been laid to rest here. Rabbi Pinchas Ben Yair, the son-in-law of the famed 1st-century Rabbi Shimon Bar Yochai, is also buried here and a bag of prayer requests hangs from a fig tree at the base of his tomb. Tradition has it that the grave of Hannah and her seven sons, who refused to renounce their religion and were executed (probably around 166 BC), is also somewhere in the cemetery. Blue and white tombstones decorated with bright flowers make it a serene and relaxing place to visit and the thousands of devout visitors add to its mystical air.

Synagogues

All the synagogues listed below are located in the Old City of Tzfat, amid the delightful medley of cobbled lanes and buildings. Modest dress is required to enter all, including head coverings for men.

Abuhav Synagogue

The pretty white-walled synagogue with its blue window frames is quintessentially Tzfat and is famed as being the home of the city's oldest Torah scroll. The sacred scroll is housed in one of the three arks within the synagogue and brought out three times a year: on Yom Kippur, Shavuot and Rosh HaShana. The synagogue is also the site of several miracles. A violent earthquake in 1837 destroyed the entire synagogue except for the wall in which the Torah scrolls were housed (indeed, this is the only

synagogue to withstand both this and the 1759 earthquake), while in 2006, a Hezbollah rocket landed in between the Abuhav and Alsheich synagogues. Although other buildings around were destroyed, neither synagogue was affected.
Alsheich St.

Alsheich Synagogue

This synagogue is named after Rabbi Moshe Ben Ha'im Alsheich, who gave weekly Torah readings here. After suffering several thefts, the synagogue is now closed to visitors but the interior can be seen through the doors.
Alsheich St.

Abuhav Synagogue, home of Tzfat's oldest Torah scroll

ROSH PINA

A short distance from Tzfat, on the slopes of Mount Canaan, is the charming and almost impossibly pretty town of Rosh Pina. Wide, leafy streets are lined with luxury guesthouses and small gourmet restaurants set within family-run stone cottages with bougainvillea growing up the sides. At the top of the hill is a small maze of cobbled streets where artists' workshops offer a wide range of fascinating and creative works. In fact, only artists may purchase land in Rosh Pina, a restriction made to maintain the unique vibe. Kabbalah tradition also has it that the Messiah will appear in Rosh Pina, and renowned Kabbalah follower and pop idol, Madonna, once famously considered purchasing property here.

Ashkenazi Ari Synagogue

This is one of the best-known and most visited of the city's synagogues, named after one of the foremost Kabbalah masters – Rabbi Isaac Luria (known as Ari) – and founded by Spanish exiles in the 16th century. It is believed a miracle occurred here when, during the 1948 Arab–Israeli War, people sought shelter in the synagogue and, despite direct attacks on the building, not a single person was injured. Rabbi Isaac Luria is, alongside Rabbi Shimon Bar Yochai, the most revered Kabbalistic rabbi and is believed to have studied with Elijah the Prophet within the synagogue.
Guri HaAri St.

Beirav Synagogue

This is one of the newest and most popular synagogues in the city, and is renowned for its lively services, especially on Shabbat and during the week-long Clarinet and Klezmer Music Festival that is held in the city each July. The synagogue attracts all types of people, from the devout to tourists and secular Israelis.
Meginei Tzfat St.

Sephardic Ari Synagogue

One of the oldest-surviving synagogues in the city, this was a favourite place of prayer for Rabbi Isaac Luria (Ari).
HaAri Rd.

Yosef Caro Synagogue

Yosef Caro was a great Jewish scholar and Kabbalist who, following his expulsion from his native Spain in 1536, settled in Tzfat and became the Chief Rabbi. He is most famously accredited with writing the *Shulchan Aruch* ('The Set Table'), the basis of Jewish law. The synagogue has been twice destroyed by earthquakes in its lifetime and promptly rebuilt.
Beit Yosef St.

Yossi Bana'a Synagogue

Built by Jews emigrating from Spain in the 15th century, this synagogue is best known for housing the tomb of Rabbi Yossi Bana'a, a Talmudic sage, known also as 'the White Tzaddik' for the miracle he performed – turning a black chicken white on Yom Kippur. Within the ark is kept a Torah scroll that is taken on the eve of Lag Ba'Omer to Mount Meron.
Yud Aleph St.

Holy cities and hidden tombs

The Galilee has long been regarded as a special land. For centuries, the verdant valleys, mountain peaks, gushing rivers, dense forests, rounded hilltops and the great Sea of Galilee have drawn people by their beauty, fertility and spirituality. Great trade caravans swept down from Damascus on their way south to Egypt, and prosperous cities appeared along the route, witnesses to conquests, rebellions and countless phases of occupation throughout their long existence.

Today, the Galilee is a proverbial patchwork formed from historical events which have seen empires settled, battles fought and lost, and empires replaced. Yet beneath this ever-changing picture, in which the Romans, Crusaders, Byzantines, Ottomans and so many more took control of the land, lies the religious make-up of a complex country. For belief takes more than a battle to change, a fact proven by the Jewish people who have survived in the landscape for thousands of years. The quiet, holy Jewish sites of the Galilee are testament to this.

Within the land, four holy cities emerged over the centuries:

Jerusalem, Hebron, Tiberias and Tzfat. The latter two are located within the Galilee, and their Jewish spiritual significance is profound. Located on the slopes of Mount Canaan, Tzfat became a holy city following the huge influx of Jews expelled from their native Spain in the 15th century, but legend has it the city was originally built by one of Noah's sons after the Great Flood. Synagogues were built and it quickly became a centre of Kabbalistic learning, with Jewish scholars, sages and rabbis congregating here.

Tiberias' holy city status is due to the large influx of rabbis who together created a centre for Jewish learning in the 18th and 19th centuries. The *Talmud* (a key Judaic text) was composed here (4th–6th centuries), and according to Jewish tradition, redemption will begin in Tiberias when the Messiah rises from the sea and enters the city.

The Galilee is dotted with the tombs of prominent Jewish rabbis whose contributions to the religion are paramount. Nowhere is this more so than at the tomb of Rabbi Shimon Bar Yochai, who is credited with having written the *Zohar*, the principal script in Jewish Kabbalah. His tomb is located on the forested Mount Meron in the Upper Galilee. Once a year, thousands of Jewish pilgrims descend on this quiet mountain to commemorate two events: the anniversary of the death of Rabbi Shimon Bar Yochai and the festival of Lag Ba'omer, which fall on the same date in May. The festival, as tradition has it, celebrates the end of a great plague that struck the Jews for not respecting one another. Dancing, singing and merriment is had by all, yet it is a devout festival attended only by Orthodox Jews.

Further west in the Upper Galilee is Beit She'arim, the site of thousands of ancient tombs carved into the hillside. It was at Beit She'arim that the Sanhedrin – the Jewish school of learning – was located, headed by the revered Rabbi Yehuda HaNassi at the end of the 2nd century AD. Upon his death, news of his burial site spread and Jews came from far and wide to live and ultimately be buried next to his tomb, making it the holiest Jewish burial site throughout the Mishnaic and Talmudic periods (AD 70–500).

Nestled into the alpine forests of the Upper Galilee is Bar'am National Park, usually off the main tourist trail but with a significant history and the privilege of being home to one of the most beautiful ancient synagogues in the country. Legend has it that the synagogue was built here in honour of Queen Esther, for whom the festival of Purim is celebrated.

Tzfat cemetery

Golan Heights

According to UN classification, the Golan Heights are Israeli-occupied. In 1981, Israel incorporated the region into its territory, an act not recognised by the international community. It therefore continues to be a disputed zone. Its inclusion in this guide is due to its tourist appeal only, and is no reflection of the political views held by either the author or Thomas Cook.

The Golan Heights are some of the most remote, undeveloped and ruggedly beautiful areas of the country and, for those with the time, hugely rewarding. Green slopes rise from the shores of the Sea of Galilee to the uplands of the southern Golan Heights, where villages and kibbutzim are sprinkled across the landscape, fat, healthy cattle graze on the land and rural tourism is booming. Transport networks are sparse, urban trappings obsolete and shopping ventures impossible. Yet because of all that, this region is one of the most alluring and unique in the country and offers a wealth of wild landscapes and rural activities.

The northern region, however, is different, both in character and looks. It is characterised by jagged peaks, gushing rivers and waterfalls, Druze communities and eagles soaring in the skies above crumbling Crusader castles. Landmines and bullet-ridden, long-abandoned buildings are lasting reminders of the violent past of the region, yet its wild beauty is unparalleled.

While there is a skeleton transport network in the Golan Heights, waiting around for sporadic buses is time-consuming and if you want to get off the main roads to explore (outside landmine territory, of course!), you will want to take a car, which obviously allows for a lot more independence and flexibility.

South Golan Heights
Hamat Gader

For thousands of years, hot thermal springs have poured out of the ground at this site in the southernmost Golan Heights. Archaeological evidence tells us the site was inhabited from the 2nd to 9th centuries AD, when people were drawn by the therapeutic properties of the springs. This continues to be the case today, and the sulphur-smelling hot springs of Hamat Gader have been developed into a hugely popular spa,

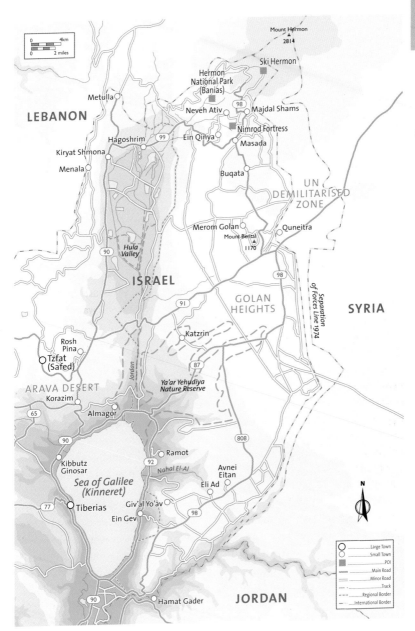

with countless pools, a lush hotel and even a rather unusual alligator park. It can get terribly crowded in summer and on weekends, so visitors are recommended to avoid visiting at these times.

Tel: (04) 665 9964. www.hamat-gader.com. Open: Mon–Fri 8.30am–10pm, Sat & Sun 8.30am–5pm. Admission charge. Bus: 24 (leaves Tiberias once a day at 9.15am & returns at 3.15pm).

Katzrin

If there is anything that could be described as an urban centre in the southern Golan Heights, then Katzrin is it. The few buses that traverse the region pass through here; there are two small shopping centres and some basic facilities and services. There isn't a lot

Ruins at Katzrin

to see or do, and it isn't particularly attractive, especially compared with the rural villages around it, but it is a practical hub for the area and so it is likely you will pass through at some point.

About 2km (1¼ miles) from the town is a new centre which contains the tourist information office, banks and ATMs, and a few pubs and restaurants. It is also home to **Golan Magic**, a multi-sensory 180-degree film depicting the colourful history and geography of the Golan Heights. Between the shopping centre and the town is the **Katzrin Ancient Village**, a large-scale reconstruction of a Talmudic village and synagogue. It was built on the site of a previous village that was destroyed in the earthquake of AD 746. It includes residential buildings and olive and wine presses, and helps visitors imagine how many of the surrounding archaeological ruins of the Galilee and Golan Heights would have originally appeared. Also of interest is the Golan Archaeological Museum located in the town itself, which has displays ranging from prehistory through to Talmudic times (AD 70–500).

Golan Magic. Tel: (04) 696 3625. www.magic-golan.co.il. Open: Sun–Thur 9am–5pm, Fri 9am–4pm, Sat 9am–5pm. Admission charge.

Golan Archaeological Museum. Tel: (04) 696 1350. Open: Sun–Thur 9am–4pm, Fri 9am–3.30pm, Sat 10.30am–1.30pm. Admission charge.

Sensational views from Mount Bental

Katzrin Ancient Village. Katzrin Rd East. Tel: (04) 696 2142. www.parkqatzrin.org. il. Open: Sun–Thur 9am–4pm, Fri 9am– 2pm, Sat 10am–4pm. Admission charge.

For Katzrin town, Bus 966 leaves Jerusalem twice a day at 8.45am & 5.15pm & returns at 6am & 1pm; Bus 55 leaves Katzrin at 11.30am for Kiryat Shmona & stops at all major villages in the northern region; Buses 15 & 19 go between Tiberias & Katzrin around the Sea of Galilee three times a day.

Mount Bental and Merom Golan
At 1,170m (3,838ft) high, **Mount Bental** towers over the surrounding landscape. Its obvious vantage and strategic prowess over neighbouring Syria made it an important factor in the 1973 Yom Kippur War and Israel's capture of the Golan Heights. The

summit has been turned into a poignant memorial for one of the war's bloodiest battles, which occurred in the valley below – known as the Valley of Tears. A bunker and base allow visitors to explore the old military unit, and in the valley, now within the UN Demilitarised Zone separating the Golan Heights and Syria, are the uninhabited remains of **Quneitra**, the Syrian village at the heart of the battle.

At the base of the mountain is the picturesque little kibbutz of **Merom Golan**. The kibbutz is home to a renowned meat restaurant and lovely guest cabins, and offers a host of rural activities. The horse-riding centre in particular is excellently run and very popular. Jeep and ATV tours, a communal swimming pool and a great central location in the Golan Heights make this a good base.

Bus 55 leaves at 12.15pm for Kiryat Shmona, Bus 58 leaves at 5.30pm for Katzrin.

Ramot

Ramot is the epitome of the southern Golan. The tiny village overlooking the Sea of Galilee is awash with family-run cabins, rustic gourmet restaurants and outdoor activity opportunities, with myriad hand-painted wooden signs directing visitors to these. Horse-riding treks, 4WD tours and bicycle rentals are all on offer, and the village is well positioned to allow exploration of all the surrounding national parks such as Ya'ar Yehudiya (see below), the Kursi archaeological site and Nahal El-Al, a lovely river walk with two waterfalls. *Buses 15 & 22 from Tiberias make the journey a few times a day.*

Ya'ar Yehudiya Nature Reserve

This nature reserve is undoubtedly one of Israel's finest parks and covers a vast portion of the southern Golan Heights. It stretches out in the shape of five fingers, with waterfalls, valleys, streams and pools. An abundance of flora and fauna can be found within the landscape, ranging from vultures and eagles to jackals, red foxes and wild boar. The Meshushim Pools are one of the top attractions and can be accessed from either side of the park. These unusual geological features are comprised of pentagonal-shaped columns around clear pools, and even the hike to reach them is delightful.

LANDMINES

Signs abound in the landscape of the northern Golan Heights, warning motorists and would-be hikers to beware of landmines. It comes as a shock to many visitors to see these signs along the edges of the roads, but it must be remembered that not so long ago this region saw bloody battles and violent wars, and remnants of these have been left behind. In addition, the IDF (Israel Defense Forces) do training up here, so don't be alarmed to see tanks chugging across the distant hills. Pay heed to warning signs though, and don't venture off-road.

There are countless excellent hiking trails within the park, and the national park offices can supply maps and route ideas. Note that some of the routes are extremely challenging, so it is important to know what you're getting into before setting off. There is a campsite next to the offices for those wanting to get an early start. (*For a recommended walk, see pp114–15.*) *Route 87. Tel: (06) 696 2817. www.parks.org.il. Open: daily 8am–5pm (closes one hour earlier in winter). Admission charge. Bus: 15 (Tiberias– Katzrin) stops at the junction near the park offices.*

North Golan Heights
Druze villages

On the lower slopes of Mount Hermon are the small towns (or big villages) of Majdal Shams, Masada, Ein Qinya and Buqata, with Majdal Shams and Masada being by far the biggest of these. (Masada is pronounced 'masadeh' and is not to be confused with the archaeological site of Masada, pronounced 'metzada', on the Dead Sea, *see pp124–5.*) The villages are inhabited by Druze communities whose hospitality, traditional foods and colourful markets are known across the country. Agriculture forms the core of industry in the villages, and young shepherds herd their goats through town, farmers on horseback clip-clop along the streets, and tractors pull trailers laden with fresh fruit and olives. Yet the towns are relatively affluent, and new cars and modern houses are commonplace.

For visitors to the area, the Druze villages are not particularly beautiful or at first sight appealing. Yet the fascinating culture of the people who live there is best observed through people-watching from one of the small, rustic eateries on the main street. Home-made sumptuous hummus, *labane* cheese, freshly picked and pickled olives, and tender meats are served with a smile and genuine hospitality.

The story of the Druze families who live in the Golan Heights is a sad one. After the 1967 Six-Day War, Israel controlled much of the area, having captured it from Syria. The Druze communities that were scattered across the landscape all of a sudden found themselves cut off from neighbouring villages, some ending up on the Israeli-controlled side and others still in Syria. Israel and Syria have not had, since that time, any communication – including

telephone, mail or border crossings – so until the advent of mobile phones and the Internet, the Druze people could only communicate by way of a hill just outside Majdal Shams. Known as the Shouting Hill, it was here that families would gather for weddings, funerals and important days to shout messages through megaphones to their loved ones on the other side. Yet the Druze are not bitter. A peaceful folk, they have adopted the nationality of the country in which they live, and men even serve voluntarily in the IDF.

Hermon National Park (Banias)
The Hermon National Park (generally simply referred to as Banias) has its lion's share of alpine beauty and archaeological interest, and makes for a very pleasant day out. The spring that

The peaks of Mount Hermon

Alpine scenes on Mount Hermon

Great. Later, his son, Philip, built his capital here. Named Caesarea Philippi, it became an important Christian pilgrimage site. A marked trail leads from the waterfalls past the cave and to Roman and Crusader remains, forming a loop through the landscape (90 minutes). There are several options for more strenuous, longer hikes which the park offices can advise you on. *Tel: (04) 695 0272. www.parks.org.il. Open: Sat–Thur 8am–5pm, Fri 8am–4pm. Admission charge. Bus 55 leaves Kiryat Shmona once a day at 1.30pm & Bus 58 at 4.40pm, & both stop outside the park entrance.*

Mount Hermon

When you think of the Middle East, ski resorts are probably one of the last things to spring to mind. Yet the towering Mount Hermon is home to the country's only ski resort – albeit a small one with, in recent years, not a whole lot of snow. Mount Hermon has long played a crucial strategic role in the defence of the Golan Heights, and an important military base is located on its 2,224m (7,296ft)-high summit, giving it the nickname 'the eyes of the nation'. The mountain is scenically spectacular, towering above the villages that are sprinkled over its lower slopes. A drive up the winding road offers incredible views – and a distinct drop in temperature, so take some warm attire. There is an unarguably alpine feel here, where meltwater rivers and waterfalls tumble down to the valleys

feeds the park begins at the foot of Mount Hermon, where meltwater pours down from the almost year-round snow-capped peak. As it runs down the steep slopes of the mountain it enters a canyon-like gully and comes crashing out into the national park in the form of an impressive waterfall. Considered to be one of the most beautiful in Israel, the waterfall is at its strongest in April and May. From here, the Banias Stream meets the Dan River and together they form the Jordan River.

A stepped path near the spring leads to a cave, in front of which are the remains of a temple built by Herod the below and where the air is crisp and fresh (and in winter downright cold). *Ski resort. Tel: (04) 698 1333. www.skihermon.co.il. Admission charge. There is no public transport up the mountain.*

Nimrod Fortress

As the sun sets over the Golan Heights, the last thing it illuminates is the hill upon which the crumbling remains of the Nimrod Fortress stand. Located on the ancient road to Damascus, it was a crucial strategic and defensive point in the Holy Land during the Crusader era, and was constructed by Al-Aziz Uthman, Saladin's nephew, in an attempt to stop the Sixth Crusade reaching Damascus from their capital in Akko. The castle was later extended and refortified by the Mamluk sultan Baibars and, following the collapse of the Crusades in Akko, it fell into ruins. Today, it offers truly breathtaking views over the northern Galilee and Golan Heights landscape and is a worthwhile place to spend a couple of hours exploring.

Tel: (04) 694 9277. www.parks.org.il. Open: daily 8am–5pm. Admission charge. Bus 55 leaves Neve Ativ for Kiryat Shmona at 12.45pm & stops at the entrance to the fortress.

The crumbling remains of the Nimrod Fortress

Walk: Ya'ar Yehudiya Nature Reserve

This is one of the most challenging, entertaining and beautiful walks in the Golan Heights, traversing archaeological ruins, high plateaux, valleys and waterfalls. Yet it isn't a gentle stroll in the countryside and involves some clambering down steep cliffs and wading and swimming through deep pools.

Those that embark on this walk should be prepared to get wet from head to foot, and take precautions with their belongings (watertight bags or some form of floating device to put backpacks on will be needed), as well as wearing sturdy footwear that they don't mind getting wet (not flip-flops).

The 4km (2½-mile) hike takes approximately three to four hours.

Begin at the Ya'ar Yehudiya Nature Reserve office on Route 89. Cross the main road away from the offices (from where you can pick up excellent hiking maps of the area) and head off on the red-marked trail eastwards. At this stage you will be on the ridge of Nahal Yehudiya.

1 Nahal Yehudiya

On this ridge it is possible to see vultures and eagles soaring overhead. *Still at the top of the ridge and a short way into the hike you will come across* the remains of an ancient settlement, thought to be the city of Sogane.

2 Sogane

Sogane is recorded in sources as being one of the Jewish cities that Josephus Flavius fortified in preparation for a revolt against the Romans (*see p116*).

From the ruins, green and red paths lead off in different directions. Follow the red trail along the edge of the canyon, which offers lovely views towards the Sea of Galilee.

3 Yehudiya Waterfall

Gradually, the trail leads down into the valley to the base of the Yehudiya Waterfall where a lovely pool offers the opportunity for a refreshing swim. Here, the vegetation changes from the sparse trees and grass pastures of the plateau to the lush greenery of the valley, where date palms, fig trees and pink oleander bushes add scent and colour.

From the waterfall, continue down the red trail (along which you will need to climb down a small shelf) until you reach the second waterfall about half a kilometre (¼ mile) away.

4 The second waterfall

When you arrive at the shelf of the waterfall, a metal ladder leads 9m (30ft) down the side of the waterfall straight into the pool below. When you reach the final rung, be prepared to swim across the deep water to the other side. Once on the other side, another climb will drop you into a shallower pool where you can wade to the other side.

From the second waterfall, follow the Yehudiya Stream southwards.

5 Yehudiya Stream

The path weaves its way downhill in the direction of the Sea of Galilee, criss-crossing from one side of the stream and pools to the other. Expect to get wet as you swim or wade across this stretch of water, or you can opt to clamber over the rocks fringed by wild flowers.

After following the stream for 1km (²⁄₃ mile), the green-marked trail leads out on to the main road while the red-marked trail continues south, adding another three hours on to the hike. The green trail will lead you back the way you came. You will emerge next to the abandoned village a short distance from the national park offices.

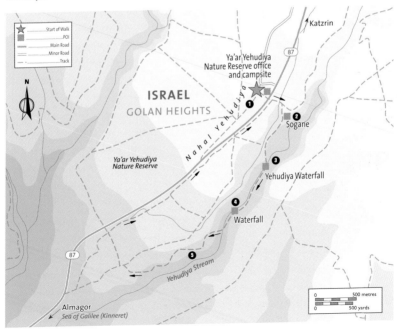

A disputed land

The small stretch of land that comprises the Golan Heights has seen its share of drama and violence over the centuries. The site of bloody wars and battles, it sits unwittingly on a prime strategic point, its elevation, water supply and position on the crossroads of ancient empires and modern countries, making it a valuable prize.

Between 953 and 586 BC, the land was contested by the ancient Kingdom of Israel and the Aramean Kingdom in Damascus until, in 332 BC, Alexander the Great conquered the entire region, and it became heavily settled. It changed hands once again when the Romans conquered the Holy Land, and during this time great cities such as Banias, Gamla, Hippos and Gadera flourished here. That is until the great Jewish revolts began against Roman rule, when fierce battles ensued, such as the one at Gamla, the capital of Jewish Golan. Under Commander of the Galilee, Josephus Flavius, the residents of the fortified city fought Roman troops in a bloody revolt that ended with the slaughter of all Jewish inhabitants.

Following the defeat of the Byzantines, the region fell to the Syrians and was all but forgotten until the Crusader period, when the route from the Holy Land to Damascus passed through these parts. The great castles that were built saw many battles between the Crusaders and Muslims.

In the 16th century, the Golan Heights was incorporated into the Ottoman Empire and remained so until it was included in the French Mandate of Syria during the dissolution of the Middle East after World War I. The declaration of the State of Israel on 14 May 1948 resulted in the fierce 1948–9 Arab–Israeli War, throughout which the Golan Heights played an important strategic role for the Syrians, who fired on Israeli troops from their elevated positions. The Israelis, for their part, diverted the crucial water sources into Israel and away from Syria. Border skirmishes continued until the 1967 Six-Day War, which saw Israel capture the Golan Heights (as well as Egypt's Sinai Peninsula and the West Bank and Gaza Strip). Since then there have been countless attempts by the Syrians to reclaim their land, including the violent and bloody 1973 Yom Kippur War, but to no avail. While Sinai was returned to Egypt, the critical defensive position of Mount Hermon left the Israelis unwilling to hand over the Golan Heights, and a long-standing stalemate has ensued. Indeed, the Golan Heights has become the stumbling block of any potential peace negotiations between the two countries, and a United Nations Disengagement Observer Force has been in place to maintain a ceasefire. Its hankering for its captured lands has seen Syria ally itself with militant anti-Israel groups such as Hezbollah and Hamas, as well as Iran, with devastating consequences over the years, including suicide bombings, rocket attacks and wars.

In 1981, Israel annexed the Golan Heights and incorporated it into the State of Israel, a controversial move that was not accepted by the UN nor the international community. Today, it is defined as an occupied land.

Scars of the past are scattered across the landscape of the Golan Heights, from archaeological remains and fortresses to landmines and bullet-ridden buildings. Yet travelling around this beautiful, wild stretch of land it is hard to imagine the violence and dramas it has witnessed. For today, the quiet expanse of mountains, plateaux and rivers is a true highlight of the Middle East, whoever it belongs to.

The much-fought-over Golan Heights

The south

The entire south of Israel is desert. The Negev, Judaean and Arava deserts together form the vast lunar landscape of dusty, rugged rocks where cliffs and valleys have formed throughout thousands of years. The Dead Sea, the world's lowest point and a unique geological marvel, marks the eastern border with Jordan and provides a wealth of spa, hiking and beach opportunities, while the vast Makhtesh Ramon is a breathtaking crater that sweeps across the lower Negev Desert.

Tiny kibbutzim can be found scattered across the vast landscape, many of them having adopted revolutionary agricultural practices or converted to eco kibbutzim, a growing trend in Israel which attracts those wanting to shrug off the urban trappings of their normal lives. Desert oases such as Ein Gedi and Ein Avdat nature reserves provide a valuable source of water to the wildlife of the desert region, as well as offering spectacular walks through lush green valleys dense with flora and fauna. Ancient archaeological ruins are to be found all over the land, from the cliff-top Roman palace built by King Herod to the isolated settlements that formed the great Nabatean Spice Route. While the majority of the region is utterly rural, towns such as Beer Sheva, which acts as the gateway to the region, and Eilat, the holiday city on the shore of the Red Sea, provide leisure opportunities, services and transport links. In the heart of the Negev Desert, Mitzpe Ramon forms the hub of desert activities.

At first glance, the south of Israel may not appear to hold the wealth of appeal of the central and northern regions, but this couldn't be further from the truth. It is a ruggedly beautiful region, where nature, the outdoors, desert pursuits and eco adventures prevail.

Negev Desert

The Negev Desert comes as a surprise to many who arrive expecting the rolling sand dunes of the Sahara. The region is characterised by a craggy, rocky landscape dotted with oases, small villages or kibbutzim, peaks and valleys, and gargantuan craters. Covering a vast 12,000sq km (7,500sq miles), it offers a wealth of appeal to those wanting to experience the rugged beauty and fascinating history of the Nabatean Spice Route and the eco-friendly activities on offer here.

Avdat and Ein Avdat national parks

Located just south of Kibbutz Sde Boker (*see pp121–2*) are these two

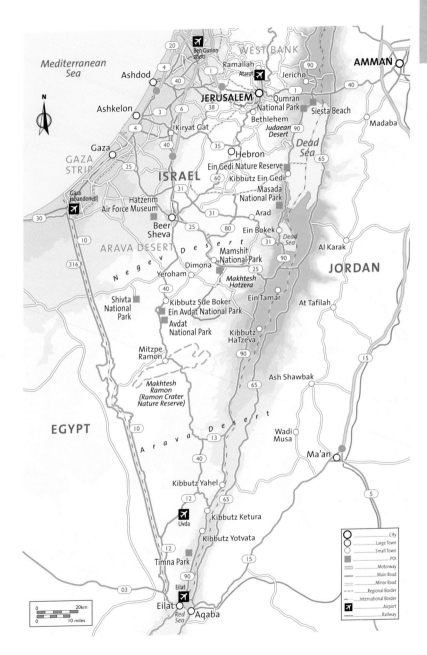

Mediterranean
Sea

WEST BANK

AMMAN

Ben Gurion 2000

N

Ashdod

Ramallah
Atarot

Jericho

Ashkelon

JERUSALEM

Qumran

Siesta Beach

Madaba

Kiryat Gat

Bethlehem
Judaean
Desert

Gaza

GAZA
STRIP

Hebron

Dead
Sea

Gaza
(abandoned)

ISRAEL

Ein Gedi Nature Reserve
Kibbutz Ein Gedi
Masada
National Park

Hatzerim
Air Force Museum

ARAVA DESERT

Arad

Beer
Sheva

Ein Bokek
Dead
Sea

Al Karak

Mamshit
National Park

Dimona

JORDAN

Yeroham

Makhtesh
Hatzera

Shivta
National
Park

Kibbutz Sde Boker
Ein Avdat National Park

Ein Tamar

At Tafilah

Avdat
National Park

Kibbutz
HaTzeva

Mitzpe
Ramon

Makhtesh
Ramon
(Ramon Crater
Nature Reserve)

Ash Shawbak

EGYPT

Wadi
Musa

Ma'an

Kibbutz Yahel

Uvda

Kibbutz Ketura

Kibbutz Yotvata

Timna Park

Eilat

Eilat
Red Sea

Aqaba

○	City
○	Large Town
○	Small Town
■	POI
	Motorway
	Main Road
	Minor Road
	Regional Border
	International Border
✈	Airport
	Railway

0   20km
0   10 miles

ecologically and archaeologically interesting national parks. Avdat National Park is well known for its importance to the ancient Nabatean Spice Route (*see pp126–7*), for the ancient hilltop settlement was one of the main stops for the great trade caravans arriving from the Arabian Peninsula on their way to the port city of Gaza. The ruins are impressive, as is the view from the top of the hill.

Nearby is the similarly named Ein Avdat National Park. With the Zin Stream and canyon at its heart, Ein Avdat is a verdant desert oasis, the scarce water supply in the area encouraging flora and fauna to flourish here. Pools, a small waterfall, springs, plenty of easy hikes and far fewer crowds than other better-known parks such as Ein Gedi make it an appealing option.

Avdat National Park. Tel: (08) 655 1511. www.parks.org.il. Open: Apr–Sept daily 8am–5pm; Oct–Mar daily 8am–4pm. Admission charge.
Ein Avdat National Park. Tel: (08) 653 2016. www.parks.org.il. Open: Apr–Sept daily 8am–5pm; Oct–Mar daily 8am–4pm. Admission charge. Buses: 60 & 392 run along route 40 between Beer Sheva & Mitzpe Ramon.

Beer Sheva

Beer Sheva forms the gateway to the Negev Desert and while it doesn't hold the same appeal as cities such as Haifa, Nazareth or Akko, many areas have undergone successful makeovers in recent years and the local tourist board has worked hard to promote it. It is a popular university town and major transport hub, with train links to Tel Aviv and frequent buses heading north and south.

The most interesting area to visit is the Old City which, while it doesn't boast quaint cobbled lanes and a wealth of impressive buildings, is interesting and has some nice restaurants. The area was built by the Ottomans in the 19th century, and many of the buildings are in dire need of a spruce-up. Smilansky Street has undergone just such a renovation and is the best place to see the former glory of the now slightly ramshackle neighbourhood. Located in a grand Ottoman building is the Negev Museum, which displays contemporary and Israeli and Bedouin pieces.

Abraham's Well in Beer Sheva

To the south of the Old City is the tourist information centre, which houses Abraham's Well. Beer Sheva is recorded in the Bible as the place to which Abraham and Isaac arrived in 2000 BC and dug a well, believed to be the one located here. At the time of writing, the entire site and offices were undergoing a huge renovation which is due for completion in 2012.

Beer Sheva is home to two bustling markets (both located on Eilat Road), both of which are worth visiting. The Town Market is a covered food market that is a great place to stock up on fresh produce and baked goods for picnics in the desert, while the Bedouin Market (open Thursdays) is a mixture of traditional Bedouin items and foods, as well as cheap imported goods from China. It is an interesting people-watching place where Bedouin families from surrounding camps and villages come to do their weekly shopping.
Abraham's Well. 1 Hevron St. Tel: (08) 623 4613. Admission charge.
Negev Museum. 60 HaAtzmaut St. Tel: (08) 699 3535. Open: Sun, Mon, Wed & Thur 8.30am–3.30pm, Tue 8.30am–2pm & 4–6pm, Sat 10am–2pm. Admission charge.

Hatzerim Air Force Museum
As you hear the roar of IDF fighter planes taking off overhead, you will be left in no doubt that you are near a major air force base. The base has converted a large tract of its land into a very entertaining and informative

museum, complete with presentations inside Boeing jets, dozens of fighter planes and helicopters, each with a historic story to tell, and an exhibition hall where serving personnel give guided tours.
Kibbutz Hatzerim. Tel: (08) 990 6853. www.iaf-museum.org.il. Open: Sun–Thur 8am–5pm, Fri 8am–1pm. Admission charge. Bus: 31 (from Beer Sheva central bus station).

Kibbutz Sde Boker
Remote Kibbutz Sde Boker, on Route 40, is famous as the retirement home and final resting place of Israel's first prime minister, David Ben Gurion, who encouraged Israelis to embrace the desert lands. Today, it has become an important stop for groups of school children, army recruits and tourists who come to appreciate the utterly spectacular views afforded from the tombs of Ben Gurion and his wife, Paula, and to visit Ben Gurion's house, left as it was when he and his wife lived

there. Sde Boker makes a good base for exploring the surrounding Upper Negev Desert, and has several delightful wine lodges and luxury farm guesthouses in the vicinity.

Ben Gurion's home. Tel: (08) 656 0320. Open: Sun–Thur 8.30am–4pm, Fri 8.30am–2pm, Sat 9am–3pm. Admission charge. Buses 60 & 392 run along Route 40 between Beer Sheva & Mitzpe Ramon.

Makhtesh Ramon (Ramon Crater Nature Reserve)

In fact not a crater but a unique geological phenomenon known internationally by the Hebrew word *makhtesh*, it was formed as an ancient sea that once covered this region retreated. Today, it measures a vast 45km (28 miles) long, 8km (5 miles) wide and 500m (1,640ft) deep and offers some of the most astounding views in the Middle East, as well as a wealth of hiking opportunities. There is a viewing platform in Mitzpe Ramon.

Mitzpe Ramon

The small town of Mitzpe Ramon sits in the heart of the Negev Desert on the edge of the great Makhtesh Ramon. It is the centre and hub of desert tourism, most of which comes with the word 'eco' in front. Tapping into the beauty of the desert and the wealth of activities within it, whether in the form of eco lodges, hiking, desert archery, horse treks or ATV tours, is what the residents of Mitzpe Ramon do best. Countless homes offer massage or alternative medicine treatments (the tourist information office can provide lists), an alpaca farm makes for an unusual experience, a bohemian eco lodge provides dance workshops, and surrounding desert camps give visitors the chance to become one with nature, experience communal living and learn to appreciate the barren beauty of the desert. It is a sleepy little town, but after a full day of activities or hiking in the crater, you will appreciate it.

Bus 60 to and from Beer Sheva or buses 392 & 382 which also go to Eilat.

David Ben Gurion's grave, Kibbutz Sde Boker

The Dead Sea and the Judaean Desert

The Dead Sea is one of the world's most fascinating geological phenomena. Not only is it the saltiest sea on the planet – 30 times more salty than the oceans – but it sits at the lowest point on earth on dry land: 400m (1,312ft) below sea level. Split between Jordan and Israel, it is a hot, dry cauldron fringed by rocky desert cliffs, great archaeological sites and thriving watery oases.

Floating comically in the waters of the Dead Sea is a must-do activity on any trip to the region and there are several very different beaches where this can be done. The most popular (and therefore busiest) is Ein Gedi beach, which attracts scores of noisy youngsters, complete with boom boxes and campfires, who use the campsite and toilet facilities on offer (which are free). Down at Ein Bokek is the very nice but also very busy Hordus beach, which has easy access and a pleasant sandy beach. Outside high season and weekdays, it is much quieter (and also free). Other beaches include Biankini and Siesta (both of which charge admission) at the northern end of the sea, and the very nice Mineral beach and spa located opposite Qumran.

There is more to the area than just the sea, however, and the following sights are well worth visiting. They are listed in order as they run along the Dead Sea from north to south.

Qumran National Park

The finds unearthed at Qumran are among some of the most significant in the world. Today housed within their own wing of the Israel Museum in Jerusalem are the most famous of these discoveries: the Dead Sea Scrolls, ancient biblical parchments that are 1,000 years older than any other surviving biblical text. Qumran was inhabited from the 3rd century BC to AD 68, and the 800–900 scrolls date from the end of that period and the Jewish revolt against the Romans. They were written by the Essenes, a breakaway sect of Jews who chose a pure life in the desert. The scrolls were found hidden in caves in 1947, and their close similarities to the texts of the New Testament have given rise to much theological debate.

Tel: (02) 994 2235. www.parks.org.il. Open: Apr–Sept daily 8am–5pm; Oct–Mar daily 8am–4pm. Admission charge. All buses heading to Ein Gedi (below) stop outside the national park entrance.

Ein Gedi Nature Reserve

Ein Gedi Nature Reserve is one of the country's most famous national parks, and it is easy to see why. Located on the shore of the Dead Sea, it spills through a green, fertile valley comprised of streams, waterfalls and pools, and is home to a wealth of animals and vegetation. Hyrax and the curly-horned ibex can be seen skipping across the steep slopes of the valley, and the area is a crucial stopover for birds on the great north–south migration route. The most famous residents, however, are the small numbers of elusive leopards who live in the surrounding cliffs. Four springs emerge at Ein Gedi, forming the core of the oasis and feeding the plethora of plant species that thrive along its valley. Settlers have long been drawn to this place in order to take advantage of this precious water supply. *Bus: 486 & 487 (Jerusalem), 421 (Tel Aviv), 384 (Beer Sheva) & 444 (Eilat).*

Kibbutz Ein Gedi

The kibbutz is located high on a cliff above the Dead Sea and adjacent nature reserve. It is a pretty kibbutz, adorned with palm trees and bougainvillea, and has a friendly, quiet atmosphere. A hotel, small supermarket and botanic garden add to its tourist appeal. The Nature's Creation spa here, which offers

Kibbutz Ein Gedi

massages, mud wraps, salt peeling and herbal saunas, is an understated and quieter alternative to the big resorts at Ein Bokek (*see opposite*), as is the Ein Gedi Sea of Spa located just along the coast, which has several therapeutic pools.

Ein Gedi Sea of Spa. Tel: (08) 659 4813. www.ein-gedi-co.il. Open: summer daily 8am–7pm; winter Sat–Thur 8am–5pm. Admission charge.

Masada

Perched atop a 400m (1,312ft)-high towering cliff above the the Dead Sea are the majestic ruins of Masada. The site is one of the country's most famous and a must-see on a trip to the Dead Sea region not only for its fascinating archaeology and spectacular views, but also for its place in the history books and hearts of Jews as the last remaining Jewish stronghold in the Roman-controlled land. After capturing the fortress, the Zealots – a Jewish sect – managed to hold out for seven years against repeated attacks by the Romans. When their defences were finally breached, they all committed suicide rather than face imprisonment. Today, young IDF recruits are brought here and it is an important stop on the Jewish pilgrimage route.

The great fortress was originally built as King Herod's palace, ornately and lavishly constructed in the 1st century AD, with luxurious bathhouses, a grand palace complex and even a swimming pool. The complex is huge, and an

An aerial view of the ruins at Masada

exploration of the ruins reveals a plush Roman villa, storehouses containing remains of huge jars, and eight Roman camps on the lower slopes for soldiers protecting the fortress. Archaeologists have uncovered the remains of a synagogue that they believe to be the oldest in the world, dating from the Second Temple period.

There are two ways to approach Masada; one from the Dead Sea side, and another from the direction of Arad. A cable car leads visitors up the precipitous cliff, while for the more energetic, the Roman Ramp (from the Dead Sea side) or Snake Path (from the Arad side) provide tiring but rewarding hikes to the top. At the base on the Dead Sea side is a very impressive museum complex, which houses many of the artefacts discovered here. And on the side of the cliff on the Arad side, a sound and light show makes for a unique and impressive display of the history of the site.

Tel: (08) 658 4207/8. www.parks.org.il. Open: Apr–Sept daily 8am–4pm; Oct–Mar daily 8am–5pm (one hour earlier on Fri). Admission charge. All buses going to Ein Gedi (see opposite) stop at Masada.

Ein Bokek

Ein Bokek stands out rather garishly in the midst of the serene and undeveloped Dead Sea region. For it is here that large chain hotels have gathered to tap into the hugely popular international phenomenon that is the Dead Sea and its products. The four- and five-star hotels each have their own state-of-the-art spa and treatment centres, beach access to the Dead Sea and lavish facilities, attracting scores of tourists every year. Supermarkets, restaurants, treatment clinics and souvenir shops have also popped up in this self-sufficient resort. *Bus 348 goes from Arad, & all Ein Gedi buses (see opposite) stop here also.*

Drive: The Nabatean Spice Route

The Nabateans, ancient nomadic Arabs, are best known for their most impressive city, Petra, in Jordan. The Nabateans controlled the vast flow of spices, gems and medicines that travelled from southern Arabia (Oman and Yemen) across Jordan and present-day Israel to the port city of Gaza, where they then went to Roman ports in the Mediterranean.

With the advance of the Roman Empire, this wealthy civilisation simply vanished. Within Israel, following the spice route north is a great off-the-beaten-track adventure.

The route is 150km (93 miles) long and takes around two and a half hours to drive. Allow for at least an hour at each site to explore the ruins.

Start the drive at Ein Saharonim in Makhtesh Ramon near Mitzpe Ramon.

1 Ein Saharonim

Within the giant Makhtesh Ramon Crater is this important water source and stronghold. The success of the Nabatean's control of the spice route lay in their knowledge of the crucial springs that watered the large camel trains and their merchants as they crossed the great deserts. Wildlife converges around the spring and there are lovely views from the scanty ruins at the top of the hill.

Head north on Route 40 towards Kibbutz Sde Boker for 23km (14 miles) to get to Avdat National Park.

2 Avdat National Park

Just south of Kibbutz Sde Boker (*see pp121–2*), Avdat was the most important city outside Petra and was, at various times over its long life, inhabited by the Nabateans, Romans and Byzantines.
Head north on Route 40 to the Telalim Junction. Turn left on to Route 211 and continue until you come to a small turn-off signposted on the left.

3 Shivta National Park

Located just off the main spice route and not fortified, the small agricultural town of Shivta likely fed the caravanserai that passed nearby. The Nabateans constructed sophisticated water systems here and at other sites. Many ruins here also date from the Byzantine period.
Head back to the Telalim Junction and cross over on to Route 4. At the HaNegev Junction, turn right on to Route 224,

through Yeroham and on to Route 225 to the Yokneam Junction. Turn left on to Route 206, continue to the Rotem Junction and take a left on to Route 25. Mamshit is signposted a short distance along this road on the left.

4 Mamshit National Park

Founded in the second half of the 1st century AD, Mamshit, like Shivta, is home to an advanced and complex water system. It was fortified in the 4th century and although it was one of the smallest towns along the route, it is probably the best preserved – indeed, a treasure of 10,000 coins was discovered here. It is possible to sleep here in summer in communal khan tents as the Nabateans would have done.
Tel: (08) 655 6478. www.parks.org.il. Open: daily 8am–5pm (closes one hour earlier in winter). Admission charge.

To return to your starting point, carry on along Route 25 to Dimona Junction, turn left on to Route 204 and continue south all the way to Halukim Junction. Continue south on Route 40 to Mitzpe Ramon.

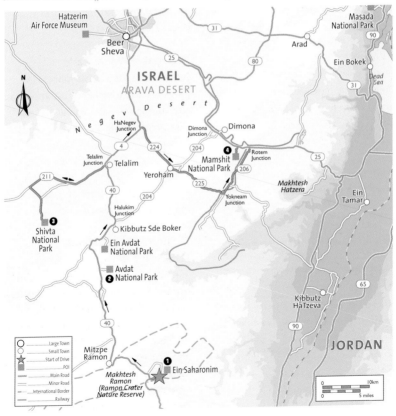

The Dead Sea phenomenon

The Dead Sea is one of the most ecologically exceptional phenomena in the world. Located in the heart of the Syrian–African Rift Valley and sitting at the earth's lowest point on dry land, 400m (1,312ft) below sea level, the Dead Sea, as the rather morbid name implies, is so salty that nothing can live in it. The waters are 30 per cent salt, making them nine times more salty than the average sea or ocean. And the Dead Sea is, in fact, not a sea at all, but a large inland lake fed in the north by the Jordan River. It measures 67km (42 miles) in length and 18km (11 miles) at its widest point, the border between Jordan and Israel splitting it almost exactly down the centre.

One of the most unexpected things about the water of the Dead Sea is its oily feel, the reason being that the water contains much more than simply salt; a dense mixture of minerals gives it not only its famed buoyancy but its therapeutic properties as well. For centuries, indeed since the days of King Herod the Great when he built a palace on a cliff above the Dead Sea, people have been drawn to the region by the healing properties of the waters. In more recent years, health spas, clinics and luxury hotels have popped up at the small resort of Ein Bokek (see p125), now the centre of a burgeoning tourist industry. Yet it isn't just the waters of the Dead Sea that are considered to be beneficial in the treatment of several health ailments such as skin and respiratory diseases. The lack of pollen, the warm, dry climate, the low radiation and barometric pressure and the mineral-rich muds found on the shores all play their part in advanced and hugely successful treatments.

CARE FOR A SALTY DIP?

Swimming or floating in the waters of the Dead Sea is a unique experience, but one that is actually much harder than it may seem! The extreme buoyancy of the water makes swimming in particular very difficult, and it is important to keep the highly saline water out of eyes. Any salt water in the eyes should instantly be rinsed with fresh water, for it can be dangerous and painful. Small cuts make themselves known as the water stings open skin, so it is best not to enter the sea if you have any major scrapes or cuts.

Don't let the cautionary warnings put you off, however. The unparalleled feeling of bobbing like a cork in healing waters surrounded by the barren beauty of the Judaean Desert shrouded in ancient and biblical history at the lowest point on earth is not to be missed.

On the back of this trend is the mass export of Dead Sea products across the world for use in the cosmetics industry. Once again tapping into the therapeutic properties of the minerals, companies such as Arava sell creams and potions in shopping centres and pharmacies across hundreds of countries.

Yet the extraction of these minerals comes at a price, and that price is evident at the southern end of the Dead Sea where evaporation pools have been created to supply the Dead Sea Salt Works. It actually isn't the beauty industry that is the root of this problem, however, as the Dead Sea Salt Works extract a variety of minerals for industrial use, including potash, bromine, caustic soda and magnesium. The water levels of the Dead Sea decrease dramatically every year and it is believed by many that by 2050 the Dead Sea may no longer exist.

A view of Jordan over the Dead Sea

Eilat and the Arava Desert

Eilat and the surrounding Arava Desert couldn't be more different. The remote, rugged and isolated desert is sparsely popoulated with kibbutzim, whose ethos of organic living has extended into a thriving but low-key tourism. Eilat, on the other hand, is ostentatious, boisterous and raucous. Popular with foreigners and holidaying Israelis alike, it is characterised by large chain hotels, Red Sea beaches and a wealth of sport and entertainment attractions.

Eilat

Eilat is Israel's holiday city. Located on the country's 7km (4^{1}/$_{3}$-mile) stretch of Red Sea coastline, it fully embraces the warm, tropical waters and year-round hot, dry climate, and has become the Holy Land's rebel city, where religious

Eilat: Israel's holiday city

observance is all but forgotten and there isn't a historic building in sight. Glitzy, luxurious hotels line the seafront promenade, restaurants of all cuisines are busy until the small hours, the bars pump out the latest tunes and the beaches are full of bronzing bodies as watersport craft zoom across the waters.

Scuba diving is big business and the calm, sheltered waters, abundant marine life and colourful corals have meant the emergence of countless dive centres. Dive cruises and day trips can be arranged to neighbouring Aqaba in Jordan and to Egypt's Sinai Peninsula through the dive centres. Jet-skis, banana boats, waterskiing and a whole host of other watersports are also hugely popular.

The Dolphin Reef is one of the city's best-loved attractions, where it is possible to watch, swim or scuba dive with several bottlenose dolphins who are famously unenclosed and free to leave whenever they wish.

To fully appreciate the essence of Eilat, spend an afternoon lazing on one of the sandy beaches. Choose from the busy town beaches or the (slightly) quieter southern beaches. Probably the most picturesque beach is the Coral Beach Reserve, whose protected waters boast thriving fish and coral species. *Coral Beach Reserve. Tel: (07) 637 6829. www.parks.org.il. Open: daily 9am–5pm. Admission charge.*
Dolphin Reef. Tel: (07) 637 5935. Email: info@dolphinreef.co.il. www.dolphinreef.co.il. Open: Sun–Thur

Solomon's Pillars in Timna Park

*9am–5pm, Fri & Sat 9am–4.30pm.
Admission charge.
Bus 15 from the central bus station heads
to the Taba border and stops along the
south shore.*

Timna Park

Just north of Eilat is the lunar-like
landscape of the 90sq km (35sq mile)
Timna Park. It is a hikers' and cyclists'
dream, with long, open roads traversing
the park, a wealth of great views, and
unique geological structures including
Solomon's Pillars and the stone
mushroom. The site is also unique in its
history and was a prosperous ancient
Egyptian copper mine (14th–12th
centuries BC), whose advanced
technologies led the way for mining
techniques throughout the region.
*Tel: (08) 631 6756. www.timna-
park.co.il. Open: Sept–Jun daily*

*8am–4pm; Jul & Aug daily 8am–1pm.
Admission charge. Bus: 397 (Beer
Sheva–Eilat).*

Yotvata Hai Bar Wildlife Reserve

This desert nature reserve is part of a
national campaign to reintroduce to the
area animals that once roamed the Holy
Land (*see p11*). It is comprised of two
sections, one a drive-through safari of
open lands where rheas, oryx, Somali
wild ass and many others freely wander,
and a small zoo inhabited by desert
species such as caracals, desert foxes,
hyenas and griffon vultures, all of
which are bred at the reserve. It is a
lovely way to get to know the fauna of
the region and see the efforts the
country is putting into its conservation.
*Tel: (08) 637 6018. www.parks.org.il.
Open: Sun–Thur 8.30am–5pm, Fri &
Sat 8.30am–4.30pm. Admission charge.*

Getting away from it all

Israel is a relatively small country, yet the scope for getting off the beaten track and away from the crowds and urban centres is vast. The Israelis are outdoor people and they love nothing more than retreating into the countryside for some rest, relaxation and an escape from hectic city life. While there is potential for getting away from it all in many places around the country, three regions stand out: the Upper Galilee, the remote desert and the Golan Heights.

Throughout the country, however, there are also certain accommodation options that cater specifically to visitors who wish to enjoy the tranquillity afforded by less populated areas, namely spas and *zimmer* (*see p144*).

Apart from those by the Dead Sea (*see p124*), which are unique unto themselves, and those in the big city hotels, there are excellent and luxurious rural spa opportunities all over the north (for those with the means), the country's most famous being Mitzpe HaYamim just outside of Tzfat (*see pp100–103*) and Hamat Gader in the southern Golan Heights (*see pp106 & 108*).

Luxury rustic accommodation in rural log cabins can also be found throughout Israel and has become somewhat of a super-trend. Known in Israel as *zimmer*, these cabins are privately owned and family-run and form the core of rural accommodation (*see p144*). They are of a consistently high standard and come at a price to match, which will usually get you a whirlpool bath, home-cooked breakfasts made of local produce, and all the quietness and serenity you could wish for.

The wild Upper Galilee

The Lower Galilee is characterised by cities, kibbutzim and villages scattered about the gently rolling green landscape. Agriculture plays a pivotal role and transport links to the rest of the country are fast and efficient. The Upper Galilee, however, offers a very different kind of landscape. Pine forests blanket the valleys and mountains, cities and towns are few and far between, and the national parks do not see the crowds of those in the southern lands. Exploring the wild landscape of this region is hugely rewarding and an excellent way to get off the pilgrimage trail and away from the urban trappings of the Mediterranean coast and big cities.

Hula Valley

Twice a year the great bird migrations head between Europe and Africa and make crucial stopovers in the Hula Valley. The large wetland landscape, with its freshwater lakes and abundant vegetation, attracts millions of birds, including 20 globally endangered species. The Hula Valley is a tranquil, relaxing place to enjoy nature at its most spectacular at any time of year, but particularly so during the migrations, when the skies fill with birds of all colours and sizes (*www.agamon-hula.co.il* has a calendar of migrations). The Agamon Hula Valley Birdwatching Reserve (*see 'Directory' listing, p180*) is a wonderful place to spend a day observing the wildlife, and Tzfat makes a good accommodation base for exploring this and other Upper Galilee sites.

Nahal Keziv

In the heart of the Upper Galilee is the sweeping Nahal Keziv, a valley fringed by the Goren pine forest, with the Keziv Stream weaving its way through the bottom. In its midst is a rocky outcrop, the crumbling, magnificent remains of the ancient Montfort Crusader castle sitting atop. Hiking through the forest and valley makes for some fabulous, albeit physically challenging, experiences as you clamber up to the ancient fortress.

In the desert

Israel is considered a forerunner in the world of ecotourism, a concept it has been implementing for decades. While Israelis certainly like the comforts of the cities, they also have a deep appreciation and respect for the natural world. The desert lands of Israel were for centuries home to nomadic Bedouin tribes, the Nabatean Spice Route once wove its way through here, and great Roman palaces were built

A view across the Sea of Galilee

Cranes in the Hula Valley

alongside the Dead Sea. Today, there is little settlement in the desert. Yet there are people who continue the tradition of desert dwelling, and those who do live there do so with a pride and dedication that is increasingly rubbing off on others. Isolated kibbutz communities are living ecologically viable lives, where sustainable building materials are used to construct houses and organic plants and fruit are cultivated in the arid soils, and a burgeoning but low-key tourism is developing on the back of all this.

Eco lodges and eco kibbutzim provide an experience like no other. It is becoming increasingly popular to escape from normal life for a week or weekend of tranquillity, gazing at a star-filled sky, sleeping in communal Bedouin-style tents (or in private cabins) and exploring the landscape. Workshops, meditation, dance, rustic cooking, treks into the desert and holistic therapies can even be found in these desert communities (*see p144*). For those less inclined to sleep alongside strangers, there are the wine lodges, where vineyards cultivated in the desert flourish and luxury cabins are offered within a setting of organic practices and beautiful, wild landscape.

Camel trekking

Known as ships of the desert, camels have for centuries been the backbone of travel and trade through the inhospitable arid lands of this part of the world. Embarking on a camel trek is a wonderful way to delve into the heart of the desert and experience it at the slow, relaxed pace that such an environment demands. As you amble over the undulating landscape, past ancient ruins, and watch as the sun sets behind the rugged cliffs, you will feel as far from the madding crowd as you could possibly be. Camel treks can range from a few hours to a week, and can be arranged in the Arava Desert through the lodges.

Golan Heights

The Golan Heights are Israel's most wild and rugged landscape, and the entire region could fall within the 'getting away from it all' category. Rolling hills, towering mountains, fresh, crisp air, grazing cattle and horse-mounted farmers make up the scenery, while Jewish and Druze villages dot the landscape, the Israel Defense Forces (IDF) train extensively in these parts, and long-abandoned buildings bear the scars of the region's volatile past. Hiking, horse riding, jeep tours, gushing waterfalls and hearty home cooking are the appeal here, and for those wanting solitude, quiet and the chance to appreciate the natural environment, the Golan Heights won't disappoint.

Hiking is particularly recommended as an easy, low-cost and thoroughly enjoyable way to experience up close the natural beauty of the area. Outside the famous Ya'ar Yehudiya Nature Reserve and Hermon National Park, one of the nicest hikes is the Nahal El-Al, which has two waterfalls known in Hebrew as the 'Black and White Falls', so named for the different rock types over which they flow. Nahal El-Al is in the southern Golan Heights near the tiny village of Avnei Eitan and is an easy afternoon walk.

Two other lovely walks both begin from the mountain-top hamlet of Nimrod and head in opposite directions. One leads southeast to Birkat Ram, a natural reservoir sitting in the crater of a dormant volcano; this walk is visible from the village and takes less than an hour. The other walk heads west into the valley of Mount Hermon and leads to the Nimrod Fortress; plan to arrive at sunset, when it is particularly spectacular.

Camel trekking is a great way to see the desert

Getting away from it all

When to go

Israel's long, hot summers and mild winters have added to its popularity as a tourist destination, and while sightseeing in the height of the summer can be sweaty and uncomfortable, there are always the wide sandy beaches at which to cool off. With twelve to thirteen hours of sunshine a day in summer and six to seven in winter, weather-wise the country can be visited almost year-round.

Israel has three distinct weather regions: the Mediterranean coast, the uplands, and the desert. The Mediterranean coast and Galilee region are characterised by long, hot, humid summers (May to September) with no rain, and very mild, rainy winters

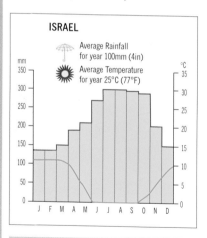

WEATHER CONVERSION CHART

25.4mm = 1 inch
°F = 1.8 × °C + 32

(November to February). The upland region, which includes Jerusalem, the eastern hills, the Golan Heights and parts of the Upper Galilee, experience less humidity and distinctly colder winters. It is not common to see snow in Jerusalem, but it does occur, and Mount Hermon in the Golan Heights has a ski resort. In both regions, rain falls almost wholly in the winter months in the form of a few heavy downpours.

The desert is extremely hot in summer, and daytime temperatures of 45°C (113°F) are not uncommon; nights are usually much cooler and more pleasant, however. In contrast to the intense humidity of the northern part of the country, the air in the desert is dry. The desert sees very little rainfall, although the non-porous ground suffers flash floods when rains do occur. Rain can fall in isolated downpours between September and April, and in winter, the desert nights can see frost on the ground.

Israel's high season falls in the summer months of May to September, when the beaches are full to bursting. The long, hot days during this season can be very tiring for those unused to such temperatures, however, and you'll find that even most of the locals are either hanging out at the beach or hiding away inside heavily air-conditioned houses. Spring (March–early May) and autumn (late September and October) are ideal for seeing the sights and spending days wandering the cobbled streets of the old cities or hiking in the national parks. The slightly cooler temperatures, lower humidity, fewer crowds, lower airfares and – in spring – the blossoms, make this an ideal time for outdoor activities and enjoying the country's nature and history.

In the desert, summers can get dangerously hot so hiking is inadvisable at this time. Again, spring and autumn are more favourable seasons. Winter nights are cold and not conducive to camping. Eilat, however, has a year-round high season, with clear blue skies and fairly constant Red Sea water temperatures of 25°C (77°F).

While experiencing some of the Jewish holidays is highly recommended, especially Yom Kippur (*see p25*) when the whole country shuts down and a quietness and tranquillity settles over the normally bustling towns and cities, the sheer number of national holidays falling around September/October can disrupt travel plans. Other religious events such as Christmas and Easter attract scores of tourists and pilgrims to Christian sites, especially those in Jerusalem, while the month of Ramadan in Muslim areas is a quiet and tranquil time. To ensure that you get the sort of holiday experience you want, therefore, it's recommended that you find out in advance which festivals or events will be taking place at the time you plan to travel.

Hapisgah Gardens in Jaffa

Getting around

Israel's public transport network is well developed, and connections between major urban areas are fast, efficient, comfortable and affordable. The main form of transport is bus, although trains are becoming increasingly popular in central regions. The country's small size means distances are easily covered, whether by public transport or car, but for more rural areas a car is the most convenient way to get around.

Bus

Buses form the core of transport options in Israel and they are excellent. A very wide network twinned with high-quality, comfortable buses makes travel throughout the country easy and stress-free. The main long-distance bus company is **Egged** (*www.egged.co.il*), and there are regional companies serving main urban areas, such as **Dan** (*www.dan.co.il*) in the Tel Aviv region. While buses connect to almost every village across Israel, services to rural areas such as the Golan Heights and desert region are sparse, so getting around takes a lot of patience and organisation. Visitors planning to explore these regions are strongly advised to hire a car.

Local bus tickets can be bought at any bus station or on the bus from the driver. They are not expensive, and ticket bundles can be purchased which cost even less. Long-distance buses can be bought online through the Egged website (which is also in English) or in

bus stations. While most don't need to be booked in advance, services such as the Tel Aviv–Eilat or Jerusalem–Eilat lines get booked up during the summer months when Israeli teenagers flock to the seaside party city, so you're best to get in early.

In terms of travel times, Tel Aviv to Haifa takes one and a half hours, Jerusalem to Tel Aviv one hour, Tel Aviv to Nazareth two hours, Jerusalem to Eilat five hours, Jerusalem to Kiryat Shmona (transport hub in Upper Galilee) three and three-quarter hours, and Tel Aviv to Beer Sheva one and a half hours. Bus and train tickets (*see below*) are fairly evenly priced, but for the most part, buses tend to be slightly cheaper and take a little longer (obvious exceptions are Tel Aviv–Ben Gurion Airport and Tel Aviv–Jerusalem).

It is also worth noting that Egged offers some good-value tours around the country ranging from one to four days. Both Egged (*www.eggedtours.com*)

and Dan also have several hop-on, hop-off city tour buses in Jerusalem, Tel Aviv and Haifa, which are a good way to see the sights.

In addition to the regular bus routes, small minivans known locally as *sherut* (shared taxi) shadow the main inter- and intra-city bus lines, offering a slightly cheaper fare and the added bonus of being able to hail them from anywhere along that route (as opposed to just at designated bus stops). They also run on Shabbat which, apart from a few services in Haifa, no other public transport in Israel does.

Train

Train travel is growing in popularity in Israel, mainly due to heavy congestion around towns and cities during rush hour, combined with ever-increasing rail services. Several lines now serve the main urban areas running from Nahariya in the far north, along the

Taxis are widely available

Getting around

Mediterranean coast, past cities such as Akko, Haifa, Netanya and Herzliya, to Tel Aviv. From there, it is possible to continue on to Ben Gurion International Airport, or change for Jerusalem. From Tel Aviv, lines continue south to the cities of Ashkelon and Beer Sheva, the gateway to the desert region. Tickets can be purchased from train station kiosks or ticket machines. Sample travel times are as follows: Tel Aviv to Haifa (one hour), Tel Aviv city centre to Ben Gurion Airport (19 minutes), Jerusalem to Tel Aviv (one and a half hours) and Tel Aviv to Beer Sheva (one and a half hours).

While there are two subways planned for Jerusalem and Tel Aviv, currently Israel's only subway system is in Haifa, where The Carmelit, as it is known, makes five stops in its traverse of the steep topography of the city centre.

Air

Because of Israel's small size, domestic flights are not hugely popular and can actually end up taking as long as the bus when you factor in security and boarding procedures. They can also be quite expensive, although the airlines often have special offers which can be very reasonable indeed. The main airports are in Haifa, Tel Aviv (Ben Gurion International and Sde Dov) and Eilat, with the latter being the city most domestic flights will serve (from Tel Aviv, Haifa is a mere hour by train, but buses to Eilat take approximately six

hours). The main airlines offering this domestic route are **El-Al** (*Tel: (03) 971 6111. www.elal.co.il*), **Arkia** (*Tel: (03) 690 2222. www.arkia.co.il*) *and* **Israir** (*Tel: (03) 795 5777. www.israir airlines.com*).

Taxi

Taxis are widely available, can be telephoned for or hailed from the street, and fares are calculated by a meter. Note that it is not uncommon for taxi drivers to try to negotiate a fare with foreigners and not use the meter; should they refuse to set it, get out and find another taxi, since they will undoubtedly be trying to over-charge you. Within the cities, fares start at 9.10NIS and the average ride costs around 20NIS; while a percentage tip is not required, it is customary to round up to the nearest shekel. Taxis do run on Shabbat, but are 25 per cent more expensive than at other times. The same applies to night fares, which begin at 9pm and end at 5.30am. It is also normal to charge 2.90NIS extra for each suitcase. Shared taxis are available which follow the main bus lines (*see p139*).

Car

Almost all major car-hire companies are represented in Israel, as well as several good local companies, the biggest being **Eldan** (*www.eldan.co.il*), and offices for all of these can be found in Ben Gurion International Airport and in most city centres. To rent a car, drivers must be over 21 years of age and be in possession of an international driving licence and credit card.

Driving in Israel involves lots of horn-honking and frustrated arm gestures, and driving techniques can sometimes leave something to be desired, especially on motorways where speed limits are rarely abided by. In general, however, road conditions are good and navigating easy, since road signs are in Hebrew, Arabic and English. It is illegal to drive without wearing a seatbelt, and only hands-free

kits may be used for talking on mobile phones. Driving is on the right-hand side of the road.

Sea

Despite boasting four seas (the Mediterranean, Sea of Galilee, Dead Sea and Red Sea), Israel has very little transportation by boat. The Sea of Galilee has tour boats and occasionally operates ferries from one side of the lake to the other, and the Red Sea offers day cruises and party boats but no ferries.

Camels and coaches at Mount Zion, Jerusalem

Accommodation

Israel is brimming with high-quality and varied accommodation, from luxury spa hotels and hip guesthouses to yurt tents and desert eco-lodges. The only downside is the price, and while mid-range or budget accommodation is growing in popularity, finding such options is considerably harder than locating four- and five-star hotel chains. Israelis love camping, however, so you never need look too far for a well-equipped campsite.

Hotels

Israel's hotels are of a high calibre and despite the sheer number of them, are full to bursting come the height of the summer. Many of the big, international hotel chains are represented throughout the country, including Hilton, Sheraton and, more recently, Leonardo, as well as national chains such as Fattal, Isrotel, Rimonim and Dan. Many cater to big tour groups, especially in places of religious significance, although there are plenty of excellent smaller hotels too. Israel's independent hotels display a creativity and level of taste seen in few other places in the world. They offer unusual buildings, themes, décor and luxury spas to an appreciative clientele, and the emergence of 'boutique' Art Deco hotels has also been hugely well received. The country's most famous hotel is undoubtedly Jerusalem's King David Hotel, the elegance of which is bettered only by its fascinating and turbulent history (*see p167*).

The higher-end establishments certainly offer high-quality accommodation but they are extremely pricey. Not all hotels offer such consistent standards. Two- and three-star hotels, however, are usually clean and comfortable and offer a variety of services and facilities.

In a small pocket along the southern portion of the Dead Sea shore is a collection of large, plush spa hotels, which have tapped into the worldwide popularity of Dead Sea products as therapeutic and beauty treatments; as the local saying goes, 'a dip in the Dead Sea takes ten years off you'. These huge hotels cater mainly to foreigners and offer all manner of clinics and spas as well as easy access to the Dead Sea itself.

Hostels

Hostels for a long time were limited to those belonging to the Hostelling International group and were frequented by groups of Israeli schoolchildren. Now, thanks to Israel's newly found place on the backpacker and independent traveller trail, more and more good-quality hostels and guesthouses are emerging on to the accommodation scene. While Hostelling International establishments (which require the purchase of a membership card) still hold at least a half share of the hostel market, independent hostels can now be found not only in the big tourist-popular centres such as Jerusalem, Tel Aviv, Haifa, Tiberias, Tzfat, Nazareth, Eilat and Akko, but in rural, isolated locales, from the Golan Heights to the desert. The bulk of these belong to the **ILH-Israel Hostels** (*www.hostels-israel.com*) group, which is an organisation of independently owned hostels within the country, and to date has 30 members. Private rooms as well as dormitories, services including Internet, Wi-Fi, bicycle hire and tour booking, and locations in some of the country's most picturesque or historic areas make them a great addition to the country's tourist infrastructure.

Luxury hotels line the seafront at Eilat

Zimmer

Israelis have managed to combine two of their greatest passions – the outdoors and being pampered – into one weekend activity: staying in a *zimmer* (pronounced 'tzimah'). Originating from the German word for 'room', *zimmers* are essentially luxury, rural cabins or small country lodges. Privately owned and built usually in the landowner's garden or grounds, they are reminiscent of Swiss chalets and all come complete with a Jacuzzi (another Israeli passion), one or two rooms (although some can be bigger) and spectacular vistas. They range in luxury from quaint and comfortable to rustically decadent, and almost always include a breakfast of home-grown or local fresh produce.

The huge popularity of *zimmers* has seen them become a national phenomenon, and they are now to be found sprinkled in abundance over the country's most idyllic landscapes. Unfortunately, that doesn't mean the prices have become any more reasonable, although on weekdays out of high season, the rates can be more than a third cheaper. At weekends, there is usually a two-night minimum stay.

Finding a *zimmer* is easy; choosing which one you want to stay in is more difficult. There are several websites for finding and booking *zimmers*, the biggest being *www.zimmeril.com*. Alternatively, drive about the countryside through the plethora of small villages and look for signs outside – you won't have to look far.

Camping

Camping is a national hobby and in the spring and summer months (especially during school holidays and at weekends), it is tent-to-tent in most campsites around the country. Israeli families from all backgrounds come in big groups, set up large tents, light a barbecue and settle in for a few days of loud chatter and family fun. During the week and outside of school holidays, however, the campsites are

DESERT ECO LODGES

In the barren expanse of desert that forms the southern half of Israel, small kibbutzim communities thrive in their unusual surroundings. A long history and deep understanding with the desert has seen the emergence of specialised agricultural techniques in the arid soils, as well as an appreciation of the fruits of the desert lands. Dedicated to this theme of organic subsistence, several eco lodges have emerged, offering visitors the chance to be at one with nature. Handmade from locally sourced products, the lodges can vary from individual mud huts to tents to wood cabins, and while you won't find a television anywhere, there is plenty to keep you entertained, whether you want to do yoga, take therapeutic classes, join workshops or go on tours of the desert. The town of Mitzpe Ramon and the surrounding area has several of these eco lodges, while there are also a handful of kibbutzim in the Arava Desert. Many of the eco lodges are part of the **Israel Hostels** group (*www.hostels-israel.com*) which has detailed information on these lodges and links to their websites (*see also 'Directory' listings*).

serene and tranquil. Most are located in highly picturesque spots; indeed, many are found inside the national parks and come with toilet, shower and barbecue facilities as well as shade. Organised campsites can be found all over the country, from the verdant hills of the Upper Galilee and the shores of the Sea of Galilee to the desert and beaches of the Dead Sea.

The countryside right of way allows camping on any non-private stretch of land as well, but dreadful forest fires have decimated large areas of land in recent years, so it is important to be careful with barbecues and campfires.

Camping shops such as LaMetayel and Rikoshet can be found in most towns and cities, and basic barbecue equipment is sold at petrol stations during the summer months.

Mitzpe Ramon Desert Lodge

Food and drink

Israel's diverse population is reflected in its varied culinary styles, and food forms an integral part of social life, whether people are attending family gatherings or religious events or just socialising with friends. From top gourmet restaurants to sumptuous street food, the country's eclectic mesh of tastes, foods and styles is one of the undoubted highlights of a trip.

Quick eats

Cheap, more-ish and oh so tasty, quick eats in Israel are one of the great pleasures of a visit. Middle Eastern hummus and falafel form the core of fast foods. Thick, creamy hummus (puréed chickpeas) is sopped up with warm pitta bread and tastes great served with chips, olives and *labane*, a soured cream cheese. Falafel are fried balls of mashed chickpeas and herbs, served inside pitta bread with salad and tahini sauce. Whichever you choose, they are fantastic value. A popular variation on falafel is *sabich*, which replaces the falafel balls for fried aubergine and hard-boiled eggs. *Shawarma* is thinly sliced lamb slow-roasted and served in pitta with sauces and salads. For something a little lighter, try *burekas*, pastry parcels stuffed with mushrooms, cheese, potato or spinach.

Cafés

Café culture is huge and there is little that Israelis would rather do at the weekend than sit and relax at one of the outdoor cafés sipping lattes or strong Arabic coffee. Funky, artistic, chic or cosy, cafés make for a perfect spot to while away a few hours and, especially in the big cities, they are *the* place to hang out and be seen. All serve food that ranges from hearty breakfasts to sandwiches and light lunches.

Restaurants

Israel is the surprising home of some top-rated restaurants, and the standard of food generally is extremely high. Restaurants, cafés and bars rise and fall in popularity and it is not uncommon to see queues down the street for some

TIPPING

It is customary to tip 12 per cent in restaurants and cafés and Israelis tend to tip generously even if the service wasn't good (although this is not compulsory). Tipping in bars is appreciated but not expected, and it is the norm to round up to the nearest shekel in taxis.

KOSHER

'Kosher' is a term used to describe food that is prepared or served according to certain Jewish religious standards. Kosher is kept to differing degrees and while there are many rules, the main ones are:

- Certain animals, including pork and shellfish, may not be eaten.
- Meat and dairy cannot be eaten in the same meal, and different cooking and eating utensils must be used for each.
- Animals must be slaughtered in a specific way and certain parts are not permitted to be eaten.

vegetarian or indulging your carnivorous side in a steak house. For something more rustic and traditional, Druze and Arab food is highly recommended, consisting of meats, a variety of salads and sticky desserts. Most restaurants have English menus, but if they don't, waiters are very happy to translate. Israelis tend to eat late, and while restaurants open around 6 or 7pm, they don't get busy until 9pm.

Bars

Israelis love to socialise and bars are big business in the cities. Having said that, the locals don't tend to consume large quantities of alcohol, and are generally happy with a couple of beers, some fancy bar snacks (which are served all night long) and an evening with friends. Alcohol is expensive and even local beers such as Maccabi and Goldstar will cost you much more than you would pay at home for a pint.

of Tel Aviv's latest 'in' restaurants. Kosher restaurants can be found throughout the country, although more secular cities such as Tel Aviv have considerably fewer kosher restaurants than pilgrimage capitals such as Jerusalem. In terms of culinary style, all manner can be found, whether you feel like going to a sushi bar, sampling French gourmet, eating organic

Night time at a café in Haifa

The Israel National Trail

The Israel National Trail is a mammoth hiking trail that traverses the entire length of the country, and is soon to be teamed with a matching and long-awaited bike trail. Inspiration for the trail came from Avraham Tamir, a well-known children's author who, at the age of 78, hiked the Appalachian Trail. Upon returning to Israel, he proposed to the Society for the Protection of Nature in Israel (SPNI) a hiking trail that would weave its way from one end of the country to the other. And so, in 1991, was born the Israel National Trail (INT). It begins in the far north of the country, where Israel hugs the border with Lebanon, the tiny Kibbutz Dan marking the starting point. The finishing line is some 950km (500 miles) further south, where Israel's Red Sea coast stops at the border with Egypt.

To undertake the entire trail takes seasoned hikers 30–45 days (maintaining a pace of 32km/20 miles a day), although a more relaxed timeframe of 60 days allows for venturing off the trail and exploring the country's national parks, religious and archaeological sites, and nearby cities. For those who embark on the entire hike, timing is everything. Israel stands between the cold steppes of Europe and the desert lands of the Syrian–African Rift Valley, creating a varied land that boasts more species of flora and fauna than anywhere else in the region. However, it is this varied landscape and climate that can be testing for hikers, and it is recommended to begin the long trek south between March and May to avoid the blistering mid-summer sun of the Negev and Arava deserts. Autumn starts are also possible but expect cooler temperatures at night, especially around the Jerusalem mountains, where temperatures can get as low as 6°C (43°F).

From the northernmost tip of the Galilee, the trail heads down through the Hula Valley, past Crusader fortresses and the tombs of Judaism's holiest rabbis to the birthplace of Jesus – Nazareth – and along the shores of the Sea of Galilee. From the Galilee, the trail takes a dramatic turn, snaking west over the undulating hills of the Mount Carmel range. Upon these hills where the Prophet Elijah battled the Priests of Baal, ancient biblical deer once again roam freely and the picturesque town of Zichron Ya'akov stands as a living memorial to Edmond de Rothschild, the grandfather of Zionism. A mesh of Jewish, Druze, Bahá'í, Christian and Muslim traditions flourish in the fun-loving, cosmopolitan towns and cities that fringe the coastline, the trail leading past the majestic ruins of the ancient port city of Caesarea, along the sands where turtles come to nest, and on to Tel Aviv. Leaving the coast behind, the trail sweeps eastwards towards the Jerusalem mountains, and while it doesn't traverse the Holy City, it comes close enough for easy visiting. The trail then sweeps down into the desert lands, past Sde Boker and Mitzpe Ramon, the renowned centres for ecotourism and desert activities, past Nabatean Spice Route ruins, remote eco lodges and the geologically fascinating Timna Park, until finally arriving in Eilat on the Red Sea.

While undertaking the entire trail is a true adventure, for those who have not the time, physical condition or inclination to embark on such a major trek, cutting the INT down into bite-sized chunks is a popular and rewarding option. *Hike the Land of Israel* contains 67 topographical maps of the trail as well as a wealth of other information and can be bought from bookshops and camping stores in Israel.
www.israelnationaltrail.com

Dramatic rock formations in the Negev desert

Entertainment

Israelis are in general a sociable bunch who take full advantage of the lifestyle their country affords them. They take seriously the adage, 'work hard, play hard', spending their free time in the city cafés and restaurants, hitting the town with friends, appreciating the flourishing art scene or just sitting back to enjoy some live music.

Cafés and restaurants

Eating out is hugely popular in Israel and you will find restaurants to suit any budget or taste. Within more secular cities such as Tel Aviv and Eilat, few are kosher and most are open throughout Shabbat. In cities such as Jerusalem and Tzfat, most are kosher and will close on Shabbat. Cafés can be found in even the most unlikely of places and Israelis aren't opposed to stopping at the petrol station for a cup of coffee. City cafés often occupy prime real estate along boulevards, seafronts and squares.

Pubs, bars and nightclubs

While Jerusalem has a decent nightlife, it is far tamer than that of cities such as Tel Aviv, Eilat or Haifa. In these cities, bars and pubs are open late, often closing when the last person heads home. Sports pubs, wine bars, cocktail bars, beach bars, gay bars, grungy pubs, pick-up bars – in Israel, the whole range can be found. Nightclubs tend to centre around the trance phenomenon,

starting late and closing in the early hours of the morning. International and Israeli DJs, such as the hugely successful Infected Mushroom, play regular gigs. Rock music also draws the crowds and many bars and pubs host live music nights, where you can hear both professional groups and up-and-coming bands. Hebrew music is enormously popular and most bars will host some sort of live music event in this genre at least weekly.

Café life in Tel Aviv

Classical and folk music

The world-renowned Israel Philharmonic Orchestra is based in Tel Aviv and plays to sell-out audiences in the Mann Auditorium. Jerusalem and Haifa also have reputable orchestras and all entertain guest conductors from around the world. The yearly Clarinet and Klezmer in the Galilee festival (*see p25*) is held in Kfar Blum and is a week of traditional, folk and classical performances, while beautiful historical and archaeological ruins, such as the Underground Crusader City in Akko, the theatre at Caesarea and countless venues throughout Jerusalem, host classical and folk concerts throughout the summer months.

Cinema

Hollywood and mainstream films are popular and there are several chains of cinema complexes which show them in English. Israeli cinema is growing within the country and beyond, and several acclaimed films have emerged, mostly on political topics. The Tel Aviv and Jerusalem cinematheques show a selection of arty pieces and have yearly film festivals.

Theatre

Theatre has long played an important role in the arts in Israel, and its style has developed from years of immigration. Countless troupes perform in Hebrew, Russian, English and French in theatres around the country. The acclaimed HaBima and

Bars are everywhere in Tel Aviv

Cameri theatres in Tel Aviv, the Khan Theatre in Jerusalem and the Haifa Municipal Theatre are among the top-rated venues.

Dance

Ballet has taken big steps in Israeli arts in recent years, thanks mostly to the Bat Sheva Dance Troupe and Suzanne Dellal Dance Academy in Tel Aviv. And classical, modern, jazz and folk dance may be seen performed in formal venues as well as less formally during festivals.

Archaeological displays

Some of Israel's best archaeological sites offer night-time audiovisual shows. Those of Masada (*see pp124–5*) and Beit She'an (*see pp92–3*) both depict the histories of the sites against the backdrop of the ruins, while Caesarea (*see pp83–5*), the Western Wall Tunnels (*see p38*) and City of David (*see p46*) all have stunning state-of-the-art multimedia presentations.

Shopping

Shopping and malls are big business in Israel; in fact, Israel has one of the highest numbers of malls per head of population in the world. For foreign visitors, however, the country's shopping charm lies not in the trendy boutiques, high-street shops or IKEA, but among the fresh fruit, vegetables and spices of the noisy, bustling outdoor markets and souks, where bargaining is allowed and indeed expected.

What to buy

Almost anything you are looking for can be found in Israel, from clothing to camping gear to toiletries to English books. Dead Sea products are one of the country's most famous exports and it is therefore unsurprising that many tourists enjoy buying these here – at great prices compared with those overseas. All big pharmacies sell Dead Sea products, and there are specialised shops in most cities and among the spa hotels along the Dead Sea. Gold and silver jewellery, Judaica, Christian religious items and arts and crafts are also popular keepsakes and collector's items. These are sold in specialist shops mainly in the old cities, at craft fairs and in the small kibbutzim and villages that populate the countryside.

Where to shop

Jerusalem

Jerusalem is home to the biggest mall in the country, the 37,000sq m (400,000sq ft) Malha Mall, located on the outskirts of the city and housing all the big-name shops such as Castro, Fox (both Israeli chains) and H&M. Foreign visitors, however, generally prefer to explore the open markets of the Old City, where religious paraphernalia, arts, crafts, jewellery and spices are displayed in a wonderful mesh of cobbled lanes. The covered Mahane Yehuda Market is an age-old institution in the city, with its daily deliveries of fresh produce and little traditional cafés (*see p44*).

Tel Aviv

Tel Aviv is the shopping hub of the country. The 1980s-style Dizengoff Center is a multi-storey mall full of mainstream shops, cafés and a wonderful Friday food fair (*see p57*). Trendy Sheinkin Street is a popular hangout filled with one-of-a-kind boutiques, hippie coffee houses and tattoo parlours (*see p61*), while other streets are great for glitzy wedding dresses, furniture, second-hand shops or Judaica. The covered Carmel Market is a colourful, busy souk filled with the scents of fresh fruit and vegetables, nuts and spices, and is a great place to practise those bargaining skills (*see p61*). And on Tuesdays and Fridays, the Nahalat Binyamin Art and Craft Fair showcases local artists' works (*see p59*).

Eilat

Eilat has long been a popular shopping destination for Israelis thanks to the fact that items are exempt from VAT here. In addition to souvenirs and Dead Sea products, electrical items – otherwise generally very expensive in Israel – are sold in large numbers in the shopping centres here. Jewellery, ceramics and textiles are also widely sold.

Haifa

Malls form the core of shopping in the relaxed city of Haifa, the Kastra and City Centre malls being the biggest and most popular.

Nazareth and Akko markets

In addition to the deservedly popular Jerusalem Old City and Tel Aviv Carmel markets, there are some wonderful, traditional souks to be found in the Old City of both Nazareth and Akko. A mish-mash of fruit and vegetable stalls, fish and meat counters, Arab bakeries, and stalls selling clothes, household items and the compulsory narghile pipes combine to form a feast of sights, sounds and scents that are quintessential to the region. Mornings are often the best time to visit the markets, especially if you're after fresh produce. Note that most Arab markets will close mid-afternoon.

Browsing at the Nahalat Binyamin Art and Craft Fair, Tel Aviv

Sport and leisure

Despite not having much success in international sporting events (with the exception of Maccabi Tel Aviv basketball club) Israelis love sport. Everything from a competitive game of bat and ball on the beach to sky-diving and kite-surfing are hugely popular. Throughout the country, sporting venues and facilities can be found at reasonable prices (or often for free) and of high quality.

In similar fashion to the Olympics or Commonwealth Games, the Maccabiah Games are held every four years in Israel, and Jewish athletes from around the world take part. The last event was in 2009 and attracted over 6,000 athletes.

Ball sports

Basketball is the passion of the country and Maccabi Tel Aviv is hugely successful internationally, having won dozens of championships, including five European cups. Tennis and basketball courts, table-tennis facilities and football pitches are widespread and most parks have one or more of the above, many offered for free.

Cycling

Cities such as Tel Aviv and Haifa have lovely seafront cycle paths, and in rural areas such as the Golan Heights, off-road cycling trips can be arranged (*see* 'Directory' for listings).

Extreme sports

Sky-diving and paragliding are the two most popular extreme sports in Israel and safety regulations are stringent, training good and equipment high quality and well maintained. Two of the biggest outfits are **Paradive** (*Tel: 170 070 2024. www.paradive.co.il)* and **Skykef** (*Tel: 170 070 5867. www.skykef. co.il*). Other listings may be found at *www.skydiveinisrael.com.*

Jeeps and ATVs are also popular, most notably in the desert around Mitzpe Ramon and the Golan Heights around Ramot and Merom Golan (*see* 'Directory' for listings).

Golf

Israel has just one golf course, the well-tended **Caesarea Golf Club** (*Tel: (04) 610 9602*).

Hiking

Apart from the famous Israel National Trail (*see pp148–9*), the range of hiking possibilities in Israel is phenomenal, and national park offices have a wealth of information. There are camping and hiking supply shops in almost every town in the country.

Rafting

The Jordan River provides the extent of the rafting opportunities, but it has become quite famous for it. The rafting centres in the Galilee (*see 'Directory' for listings*) are best visited outside school holidays.

Swimming

Community swimming pools are widespread and almost all kibbutzim have a free pool for residents and guests. Tel Aviv has the popular **Gordon Swimming Pool** (*see 'Directory' listing, p172*) but generally the beaches of the Mediterranean coast and Red Sea are the top swimming destinations.

Skiing

Somewhat surprising to many, Israel in fact has a ski resort and although it has suffered from lack of snow in recent years, it is packed with Israeli families whenever there is a flutter of snowfall. It is rather pricey and the facilities pale in comparison to any European or North American resort, but **Ski Hermon** can be a fun family activity (*see 'Directory' listing, p182*).

Watersports

Wind- and kite-surfing are big business in Israel, and the wilder strips of the Mediterranean coast and Sea of Galilee are both popular areas for these sports (particularly kite-surfing). Top destinations include Beit Yannai Beach, Bat Galim Beach in Haifa, Eilat, Caesarea and the Sea of Galilee. **Kiteaway** (*Tel: (09) 866 6991. www.kiteaway.com*) and **Kiteclub** (*Tel: (04) 855 0183. www.kiteclub.net*) are both big outfits offering tuition and rental.

Scuba diving is also very popular and Eilat forms the hub of all subaquatic activities. Courses, dives excursions and cruises to Egypt and Jordan are run through the dive centres (*see 'Directory' for listings*). **Surfpoint** (*Dolphinarium Beach. Tel: 159 956 7888*) in Tel Aviv offers a range of facilities, including surfing equipment.

On the sea in Eilat

Children

Israelis absolutely love children and your little ones will be welcomed with open arms wherever you take them. Indeed, it is common for total strangers to want to cuddle, coo over or play with your children. This may seem unusual, but it is meant in a friendly and caring way. Activities appropriate to kids are strewn around the country and there is plenty of family-friendly fun to be had.

The following are just some of the most popular ways for visitors to keep their kids entertained. For more ideas, visit *www.israelemb.org/kids*

Aquaparks and theme parks
King's City
A biblical theme park aimed at children aged about 8–15 years.
New Lagoon, Eilat. Tel: (08) 630 4444. www.kingscity.co.il. Open: Sun–Thur 9am–1am, Fri 9am–Shabbat, Sat end Shabbat–1am.

Manara Cliff
Zip-lining, rappelling, bungy dome and cable car are just some of the activities on offer. It is well supervised and suitable for children of all ages, but older kids will get the most out of a visit.
Kibbitz Manara. Tel: (04) 690 5830. www.cliff.co.il. Open: daily 9.30am–4.30pm. Admission charge.

Mini Israel
See p49.

Shefayim Water Park
Although they don't quite compare to those of Europe in terms of size or range of attractions, water parks in Israel are still great fun.
Kibbutz Shefayim. Tel: (09) 959 5756. www.waterpark.co.il. Open: summer daily 9am–6pm. Admission charge.

Museums, cinemas and theatres
Haifa International Children's Theater Festival
Held in April, the festival hosts a selection of Hebrew and other-language children's theatre productions.

IMAX 3-D
4 Yotam Rd, Eilat. Tel: (08) 636 1000. www.imaxeilat.co.il. Open: Sun–Thur 11am–midnight, Fri 11am–Shabbat, Sat 9pm–1am.

Outdoor activities
Beaches
Scuba diving, snorkelling, swimming with dolphins, boat tours and all

manner of watersports make **Eilat** the most popular family holiday spot in the country. The shores of the **Sea of Galilee** have well-equipped campsites, aquaparks and watersports and are very popular with Israeli families. And **Tel Aviv's** wide, sandy beaches offer toilet facilities, lifeguards and good shady areas, making them perfect for families, particularly those with young children.

Camping
Camping is extremely popular with Israeli families and campsites are thus well equipped and set in ideal locations around the country (*see 'Directory' for listings*).

Desert pursuits
Camel riding, archery, camping in Bedouin tents, swimming in the Dead Sea, quad-biking and even a visit to an alpaca farm are all possible in the desert regions and make for great family activities (*see 'Directory' for 'South' listings*).

Hiking and cycling
Hiking is easily undertaken in Israel's many national parks and there are countless safe cycling trails all over the country. One of the best cycling trails for children circles the Sea of Galilee. Israel's city parks are also great for taking children cycling and roller-skating, and rental shops offering kids' seats, bikes and helmets can easily be found throughout cities.

Rafting
The Jordan River is a top rafting region, especially in summer. Rafting centres tend to cater to groups of older children and teenagers (*see 'Directory' for 'Galilee' listings*).

Timna Park
This ancient copper mine is home to some impressive geological structures that never fail to enthrall kids (*see p131*).

Zoos
Jerusalem Biblical Zoo
Tel: (02) 675 0111.
www.jerusalemzoo.org.il. Open:
Sun–Thur 9am–5pm, Fri 9am–5.30pm,
Sat 10am–5pm. Admission charge.

Ramat Gan Safari Park
Tel: (03) 631 3531. www.safari.co.il.
Open: Sun–Thur 9am–7pm, Fri
9am–2pm. Admission charge.

Yotvata Hai Bar Wildlife Reserve
Route 90, Arava Desert. Tel: (08) 637
6018. www.parks.org.il. Open: Sun–Thur
8am–5pm, Fri & Sat 8.30am–4pm.
Admission charge.

Dolphin Reef, Eilat (*see p130*)

Essentials

Arriving and departing

By air

Israel's main international airport is Tel Aviv Ben Gurion Airport, although some charter flights now go to Eilat. The country's national airline is El-Al, known for its extreme security measures and serving cities across the world. Many major airlines serve Ben Gurion Airport, including most top US and European carriers, and there are increasingly more European budget airlines offering flights to Israel, including easyJet, Air Berlin and Jet2.

By land

Although Israel has borders with Lebanon, Syria, Egypt and Jordan, due to a lack of diplomatic relations, only the latter two can be crossed overland. It is also possible to travel to the West Bank, but the Gaza Strip is currently closed.

Egypt: Visas are not needed to travel to the Sinai Peninsula, but to continue on to mainland Egypt, visas must be applied for in advance at the Egyptian Consulate in Tel Aviv.
Taba Border. Tel: (08) 636 0999.
Open: 24 hours. Exit fee charged.
Jordan: Visas cannot be obtained from the border and must be applied for at the Jordanian Embassy in Tel Aviv.
Jordan River Border, Beit She'an.
Tel: (04) 609 3400. Open: Sun–Thur
8am–9pm, Fri & Sat 8am–8pm.
Exit fee charged.
Allenby/King Hussein Border. Tel: (02)
548 2600. Open: Sun–Thur 8am–8pm,
Fri & Sat 8am–3pm. Exit fee charged.
Yitzhak Rabin/Arava Border, Eilat.
Tel: (08) 630 0555. Open: Sun–Thur
6.30am–8pm, Fri & Sat 8am–8pm.
Exit fee charged.

By sea

Israel has no ferries in operation, although several major cruise lines now incorporate Israel into their itineraries. Most stop in Haifa's port.

Customs

Visitors may bring into Israel 1 litre of spirits, 2 litres of wine and 250g of tobacco. It is forbidden to bring in raw meats and plants.

Electricity

The power supply is 220V and, while sockets take type H three-pin plugs, two-pin European ones also work.

Internet

The Internet is big business in Israel. Free Wi-Fi is commonly found in cafés and hotels, and Internet cafés offer high-speed connections and good facilities. The latter tend to be found mostly in the cities, with Wi-Fi constituting the bulk of Internet access in rural areas.

Money

Israel's currency is the New Israeli Shekel (NIS). There are 100 agorot in 1 shekel, and there are 5, 10 and 50 agorot coins, and 1NIS, 5NIS and 10NIS coins. Bank notes come in denominations of 20, 50, 100 and 200. Visitors can bring unlimited sums of money into the country, and foreign currency and traveller's cheques can be cashed at the airport, exchange bureaux, banks, post offices and most hotels. ATMs are commonplace and all international credit and debit cards are accepted. Banks can be found in all towns and cities.

Opening hours

The working week is from Sunday to Thursday, and many businesses are open until early afternoon on Friday. Shabbat (the Sabbath) runs from sunset on Friday to sunset on Saturday, and many businesses close during this time. Normal opening hours for shops and businesses are 9am–6pm, although shopping centres will stay open later. Post offices and banks close on Wednesday afternoons.

Passports and visas

Citizens of the UK, US, Canada, Australia, New Zealand and South Africa do not need visas to enter Israel for up to three months, although they must be in possession of a passport valid for six months from the date of entry. Due to the state of Israel's diplomatic relations, the presence of an Israeli entry/exit stamp in your passport means you may be refused entry into Arab countries. It is now possible to ask for a 17L form, which can be stamped in lieu of your passport. Ask immigration officers on arrival into the country.

Detail from the Marc Chagall mosaic at the Knesset

Pharmacies

Pharmacies are found all over the country and stock familiar over-the-counter and prescription brands.

Post

Post-office branches can be found throughout the country and are denoted by their red and white sign displaying a gazelle. Postal services include registered mail, express and EMS (an international service) as well as poste restante. FedEx and DHL have offices in Israel.

Public holidays

Rosh HaShana	17–18 Sept 2012
	5–6 Sept 2013
Yom Kippur	26 Sept 2012
	14 Sept 2013

Sukkot	1 Oct 2012
	19 Sept 2013
Simchat Torah	8 Oct 2012
	26 Sept 2013
Pesach (Passover)	7 April 2012
First Day	25 Mar 2013
Pesach Last Day	14 April 2012
	2 April 2013
Holocaust	19 April 2012
Memorial Day	8 April 2013
National	25 April 2012
Memorial Day	15 April 2013
Independence Day	26 April 2012
	16 April 2013

Smoking

Smoking on public transport and in public buildings is illegal; people rarely abide by the law in bars and nightclubs.

Clear signposting in the Negev Desert

Essentials

Suggested reading and media

Of the many daily newspapers, *HaAretz* is published in Hebrew and English, and the *Jerusalem Post* and *International Herald Tribune* are high-circulation English papers. Over 70 per cent of houses have cable television and English programmes are subtitled, not dubbed. Israeli news channels broadcast in Hebrew but international channels can be found on cable. Radio is very popular, notably the music and news channel Gal Galatz, which is in Hebrew only but plays mostly music anyway.

In terms of fiction, Amos Oz is the most popular Israeli author today, his many titles available in English and dealing with a range of topical themes. David Grossman is another top author whose novels cover modern political issues, love and religion.

Tax

Israel has a VAT of 16 per cent, although many services aimed at tourists, including tours and hotels, are tax exempt. It is possible to claim the VAT back on purchases of over US$100 on exit through Tel Aviv International Airport upon presentation of receipts and the purchases.

Telephones

Israel has more phones per capita than any other country, and connections are extremely good even in rural areas. All hotel rooms have direct-dial phones, but these can be extremely pricey. Calling cards can be bought from newsagents and used in phone booths, and newsagents have coin-operated phones on their counters. It is possible to rent mobile phones or SIM cards from several companies that have offices in Tel Aviv International Airport. Israel's international dialling code is +972 and area codes are 02 for Jerusalem, 03 for Tel Aviv, 04 for Haifa and the north of the country, 08 for the south, and 09 for the Mediterranean coast. A new telephone provider now offers codeless numbers which, like mobile numbers, have no area code in front.

Time

Israel's time zone is GMT+2, and daylight saving is observed, although not on the same dates in April and September as most European countries.

Toilets

Public toilets are Western style and generally clean and of a good standard. They can be found in shopping centres, bus, train and petrol stations, on public beaches and in some town centres. Usually only bus stations charge for using them, and it's a small amount.

Travellers with disabilities

Israel is well geared towards travellers with disabilities, and public transport, hotels, restaurants, museums and many national parks are wheelchair-accessible and have disabled facilities. **Access Israel** (*www.aisrael.org*) can provide more detailed information.

Language

Modern Hebrew (as opposed to biblical Hebrew) and Arabic are the official languages of Israel. English is taught in schools from a young age, and many Israelis travel, so it is spoken to a high standard, especially among younger Israelis. Due to waves of immigration it is common to hear a wide variety of languages spoken in the country, including Russian, French, Spanish and Polish.

The Hebrew alphabet is comprised of 22 letters and is read from right to left. With the exception of the 'a' and 'i' sounds, the vowels are not written; materials for young children or new learners use a series of dots under consonants to denote vowel sounds; in normal written Hebrew, however, these are omitted.

Arabic is likewise written right-to-left and consists of a slightly longer alphabet of 28 letters. Like Hebrew some vowels are denoted by symbols but these are normally omitted in written Arabic.

TIME

English	Arabic pronunciation	Hebrew pronunciation
Today	el nahar dah	hayom
Yesterday	em bareh'	etmol
Tomorrow	bokra	machar
What time is it?	El sa'aa kam	ma HaSha'a?

DAYS OF THE WEEK

English	Arabic pronunciation	Hebrew pronunciation
Monday	el etnein	yom sheni
Tuesday	el talat	yom shlishi
Wednesday	el arbaa	yom revi'i
Thursday	el khamees	yom chamishi
Friday	el joma'a	yom shishi
Saturday	el sabt	shabbat
Sunday	el 'had	yom rishon

EVERYDAY EXPRESSIONS

English	Arabic pronunciation	Hebrew pronunciation
Yes/No	aywa or na'am/la	ken/lo
There is	feeh	yesh
There is not	ma feesh	ein
I want	'ayez/biddi	ani rotzeh/rotzah (m/f)
How much?	be kam	kama?
Expensive	ghaly	yakar
Cheap	rekhees	zol
Money	foloos/masary	kesef
Toilet	hammam	sherutim
Men's toilet	hammam rejaly	sherutai g'varim
Women's toilet	hammam hareemy	sherutai nashim

NUMBERS

English	Arabic pronunciation	Hebrew pronunciation
1	wahed	echad
2	etnein	shtaim
3	talata	shalosh
4	arba'a	arba
5	khamsa	chamesh
6	setta	shesh
7	saba'a	sheva
8	tamanya	shmone
9	tesa'a	tesha
10	'ashara	eser
20	'eshreen	esrim
100	meyya	mea
1000	alf	elef

GREETINGS AND COURTESIES

English	Arabic pronunciation	Hebrew pronunciation
Hello	ahlan/marhaba	shalom
Hello on the Sabbath	n/a	shabbat shalom
Goodbye	ma'a el salama	shalom
Good morning	sabah el kheir	boker tov
Good evening	masaa el kheir	erev tov
Good night	tesbah 'ala kheir	layla tov
Please	min fadlak/fadlik	bevakasha
Thank you	shokran	toda
Excuse me	la moakhza	slicha

Emergencies

Emergency numbers
For police, ambulance and fire services, dial *100*.

Medical services
Israel has a high standard of medical care on a par with North America and Western Europe, and almost everyone in the healthcare industry speaks English. The country is home to some top hospitals, such as **Ichilov** in Tel Aviv (*6 Weizmann St. Tel: (03) 697 4444*), **Hadassah** in Jerusalem (*Kiryat Hadassah. Tel: (02) 677 7111. www.hadassah.org.il*) and **Soroka** in Beer Sheva (Ben Gurion St. Tel: (08) 640 0111), although there are good hospitals in most cities. Hotels can arrange for a doctor's visit or call a local clinic; clinics which are also listed in the phone book (or pharmacies can direct you to the nearest one).

Health risks and insurance
There are no specific vaccination requirements for Israel, although it is advisable to be up-to-date with regular boosters. It may be worth considering having children immunised against measles, as there have been outbreaks in Jewish Orthodox neighbourhoods where vaccination is opted against.

The main health risks involve sun exposure, so be sure to wear sunblock, hat and sunglasses, drink plenty of water and avoid the midday sun, especially in the desert. Mosquitoes are a pest but not dangerous. In addition, there is a very minimal risk of being stung by desert scorpions or snakes; this would require immediate medical attention. Rabies also exists, but only in wild animals in rural regions.

It is important to get a good, comprehensive insurance policy for travel to Israel, as medical costs are high. Be aware, though, that while the risks of terrorism are low, most insurance policies don't cover this eventuality.

Pharmacies and opticians
Superpharm is the largest pharmacy chain store, with hundreds of branches across the country. Likewise, several chains of opticians can be found widely.

Safety and crime
Violent crime in Israel is thankfully low and most visitors don't encounter any problems. Of course, general safety precautions should be taken, such as not walking alone in unlit areas and only taking licensed taxis. Although Israel has an above-average rate of terrorism, the implementation of strict security measures means it has been on the decline in recent years. It is, however, inadvisable to venture within 12km (7½ miles) of the border with the Gaza Strip or She'ba Farms region on the Lebanon border. Note, too, that it is common to be asked to open your bag

for inspection on entering shopping centres, restaurants and the like.

Tourist police have offices in busy tourist areas such as Tel Aviv and Jerusalem Old City and usually speak excellent English.

Embassies and consulates
Australia
Embassy (Tel Aviv). *Discount Bank Tower, Level 28, 23 Yehuda HaLevi St. Tel: (03) 693 5000. Email: telaviv. embassy@dfat.gov.au. www.australian embassy.org.il. Open: Mon–Thur 8am–12.30pm & 1–4.30pm, Fri 8am–1pm.*

Canada
Embassy (Tel Aviv). *HaSapanut House, 3/5 Nirim St. Tel: (03) 636 3300. Email: taviv@international.gc.ca. www.canadainternational.gc.ca/israel. Open: Mon–Thur 8am–4.30pm, Fri 8am–1.30pm.*

New Zealand
Consulate (Tel Aviv). *3 Daniel Frish St. Tel: (03) 695 1869. Email: nzhoncon.il@gmail.com. www.nzembassy.com*

South Africa
Embassy (Ramat Gan). *Sason Hogi Tower, Floor 17, 12a Abba Hillel St. Tel: (03) 525 2566. Email: diplomatie@ ambafrance-il.org. www.safis.co.il. Open: Mon–Fri 9–11.30am, Wed also 2–3pm.*

United Kingdom
Embassy (Tel Aviv). *192 HaYarkon St. Tel: (03) 725 1222. www.ukinisrael. fco.gov.uk. Open: Mon–Thur 8am–4pm, Fri 8am–1.30pm.*

United States
Embassy (Tel Aviv). *71 HaYarkon St. Tel: (03) 519 7575. Open: Mon–Thur 8am–4pm, Fri 8am–1pm.*

Emergencies

Expect a heavy security presence in Jerusalem

Directory

Accommodation price guide

Hotel prices are based on two people sharing a room in high season.

£	Less than 250NIS
££	250–400NIS
£££	400–550NIS
££££	550–800NIS
£££££	over 800NIS

Eating out price guide

Prices are based on an average two-course meal per head, without drinks.

£	Less than 30NIS
££	30–50NIS
£££	50–70NIS
££££	70–90NIS
£££££	over 90NIS

Jerusalem

ACCOMMODATION

Abraham Hostel ££ (dorm £)

From the owners of the successful Fauzi Azar Inn in Nazareth comes this new hostel catering to independent budget travellers. Private rooms and dorms are available, as well as kitchen use, free breakfast, travel centre, games room and Wi-Fi.
67 HaNevi'im St. Tel: (02) 650 2200. Email: reservations@ abrahamhostels.com. www.abrahamhostels.com

Jaffa Gate Hostel ££ (dorm £)

In the heart of the Old City, it caters to budget travellers. Wi-Fi, lockers, barbecue area, common room and luggage storage are offered.
Jaffa Gate. Tel: (02) 627 6402. Email: jaffa_gate_ hostel@yahoo.com. www.jaffa-gate.hostel.com

Austrian Hospice £££ (dorm £)

Located in a charming building on the corner of the Via Dolorosa in the Muslim Quarter souk. Steeped in history, it offers high-ceilinged private rooms or dormitories, a lovely restaurant and café, and spectacular rooftop views.
37 Via Dolorosa. Tel: (02) 626 5800. Email: office@ austrianhospice.com. www.austrianhospice.com

Park Hotel £££

Sunny, spacious rooms have mod-cons and offer excellent value for money. Breakfast is served on the covered patio and there is Wi-Fi throughout.
2 Vilnay St. Tel: (02) 658 2222. Email: reservation@park-hotel- jerusalem.com. www.park-hotel- jerusalem.com

Gloria Hotel ££££
Excellent Old City option, housed in an old stone mansion and situated by Jaffa Gate. Spacious rooms have AC and TV and there is a bar and restaurant.
33 Latin Patriarchate St. Tel: (02) 628 2431/2. Email: gloriahl@ netvision.net.il. www.gloria-hotel.com

Knight's Palace ££££
Boasting an excellent location in a quiet alley of the Old City, this beautiful stone building with flagstone floors, arched windows and vaulted ceilings has elegant bedrooms, views of the Old City, a bar and restaurant.
Freres St. Tel: (02) 628 2537. Email: kp@actcom.co.il. www.knightspalace.com

American Colony Hotel £££££
Located in East Jerusalem, this is a beautiful example of old Jerusalem architecture and charm. Often frequented by journalists and diplomats, it has lovely grounds, an interesting history and immaculate reputation.
23 Nablus Rd. Tel: (02) 627 9777. Email: reserve@amcol.co.il. www.americancolony.com

Harmony Hotel £££££
Hugely popular Art-Deco boutique hotel in the city centre, ten minutes' walk from the Old City. A free happy hour, Wi-Fi and Israeli breakfast are included.
6 Yoel Moshe Salomon St. Tel: (02) 621 9999. www.atlas.co.il

King David £££££
Before becoming the country's most famous and elegant hotel, the King David offered asylum to exiled monarchs, was headquarters of the British Mandate authorities and was bombed by a Zionist militant group in 1946.
23 King David St. Tel: (02) 620 8888. Email: kingdavid@danhotels.com. www.danhotels.co.il

EATING OUT

Abu Shukri £
Cheap, simple hummus joint regarded as the best in Jerusalem. Located in the Muslim Quarter souk.
63 El-Wad St. Tel: (02) 627 1538. Open: 8.30am–6pm.

Pinati £
The queues attest to the long-standing popularity of this kosher falafel joint.
13 King George St. Tel: (02) 625 4540 & 057 943 8531. Open: Sun– Thur 7am–7pm, Fri 7am–before Shabbat.

Caffit ££
Kosher. A German Colony favourite, with light lunches served in the leafy courtyard. The breakfasts are particularly good.
35 Emek Refaim St. Tel: (02) 563 5284. Open: Sun–Thur 8am– 1am, Fri 7am–2pm, Sat end of Shabbat–1.30am.

Versavee Bistro, Bar & Café ££
A new addition to the Old City, Versavee serves simple but filling meals and is set within a charming 2,000-year-old building.
Greek Catholic Patriarchate Rd, Jaffa Gate. Tel: (02) 627 6160. www.versavee.com

Armenian Tavern £££
Nestled in the quiet

Armenian Quarter, this is a unique dining experience, with Armenian dishes served within an ancient, romantic cellar.
79 Armenian Orthodox Patriarchate St. Tel: (02) 627 3854. Open: Mon–Sat 11am–10pm.

Ima £££
Kosher. Located in the Mahane Yehuda Market, it serves hearty Jewish and Middle Eastern food.
189 Agripas St. Tel: (02) 624 6860. Open: Sun–Thur 11am–11pm, Fri 11am–Shabbat.

Sushi Bar Rechavia £££
A huge array of sushi, noodles, salads and soups make up the menu in this extremely popular Japanese restaurant.
29 Aza St. Tel: (02) 566 7477. Open: Sun–Thur 6pm–2am, Fri 11.30am–4.30pm, Sat 9.30pm–2am.

Blue Dolphin ££££
An old East Jerusalem favourite serving fresh fish in a Lebanese/ Mediterranean style.
7 Shimon HaTzadik St. Tel: (02) 532 2001. Open: daily noon–midnight.

Machaneyuda ££££
The latest fad in the city is this funky restaurant with a creative menu that changes daily.
10 Beit Yaakov St. Tel: (02) 533 3442. Open: Sun–Thur 6.30pm– late, Fri noon–6pm, Sat 9pm–late.

Eucalyptus £££££
Biblical foods have been created with unusual ingredients to produce an elegant, gourmet dining experience.
14 Hativat Yerushalayim St. Tel: (02) 624 4331. Open: Sun–Thur noon–midnight, Fri 10am–Shabbat, Sat end of Shabbat–late. www.the- eucalyptus.com

ENTERTAINMENT

Bolinat
Trendy bar-restaurant in the city centre.
6 Dorot Rishonim St. Tel: (02) 624 9733. Open: 24 hours.

Box offices
Bimot. *8 Shamai St. Tel: (02) 623 7000. www.bimot.co.il*
Klaim. *12 Shamai St. Tel: (02) 622 2333.*

Cellar Bar
Refined watering hole in the American Colony Hotel.
23 Nablus Rd. Tel: (02) 627 9777. Open: daily 7pm–midnight.

Egon
Bohemian-style pub with floor cushions and a relaxed vibe.
9 Nahalat Shiva St. Tel: (02) 622 2458. Open: 24 hours.

Jerusalem Cinematheque
Shows classical, avant-garde, Hollywood and experimental films in Hebrew and English.
11 Hebron Rd. Tel: (02) 672 4131. www.jer.cine.org.il

Jerusalem Performing Arts Centre
The complex includes the Jerusalem Theatre, Henry Crown Auditorium and Rebecca Crown Hall. It shows Israeli plays and holds concerts by the Jerusalem Symphony Orchestra and Israel Chamber Ensemble.
20 David Marcus St, German Colony. Tel: (02) 560 5755. www.jerusalem- theatre.co.il

Khan Theatre
Israeli and Hebrew plays, classical concerts and

folklore performances.
2 David Remez Sq.
Tel: (02) 671 8281.
www.khan.co.il
Malha Mall
Israel's largest mall, filled
with entertainment
options as well as shops.
Malha neighbourhood.
Tel: (02) 679 1333.
Open: Sun–Thur 9.30am–
10pm, Fri 9am–3pm, Sat
end Shabbat–11pm.
Mike's Place
There are live music
performances every night
and sporting events
shown on big screens at
this classic British-
style pub.
37 Jaffa St. Tel: 054 929
2551.
www.mikesplacebars.com.
Open: daily 4pm–late.
Rav Hen Cinema
Mainstream and
blockbuster movies in
English with Hebrew
subtitles.
19 Ha'uman St.
Tel: (02) 679 2799.

SPORT AND LEISURE
Hapoel Jerusalem
Basketball Club
Games are on Saturday,
Sunday and Monday
nights.
Malcha Arena.

Tel: (02) 624 1440.
Segwayz
Offers a variety of
unusual tours aboard
these motorised two-
wheeled scooters.
Tel: 052 811 9996. Email:
info@segwayz.co.il.
www.segwayz.co.il

Tel Aviv-Jaffa
ACCOMMODATION
Florentine Hostel £
(dorms £)
Great budget option in
the trendy Florentine
neighbourhood. Double
rooms and dormitories
offered, as well as Wi-Fi,
communal kitchen,
washing facilities, mobile
phone and bicycle rental,
and a barbecue area. An
age restriction of 18–40
applies.
10 Elifelet St.
Tel: (03) 518 7551. Email:
Rafi@Florentinehostel.
com.
www.florentinehostel.com
HaYarkon 48 Hostel ££
(dorms £)
Excellently geared to
independent travellers,
this hotel has a young,
lively vibe, private rooms
as well as dorms,
communal kitchen,
games, and is a stone's

throw from the beach.
48 HaYarkon St. Tel: (03)
516 8989. Email:
info@hayarkon48.com.
www.hayarkon48.com
Old Jaffa Hostel ££
(dorms £)
Steeped in Old Jaffa
charm and located near
the Jaffa Flea Market.
Private rooms and
dormitories are rustically
decorated but cosy. Free
Wi-Fi, communal
kitchen and laundry.
8 Olei Zion St. Tel: (03)
682 2370. Email:
ojhostel@shani.net.
www.telaviv-hostel.com
Maxim Hotel £££
Great-value hotel in the
centre near the beach.
Small but pretty rooms
come with AC, TV, Wi-Fi
and mini fridge, and a
breakfast buffet is
included in the room
rate.
86 HaYarkon St. Tel: (03)
517 3721. www.maxim-
htl-ta.co.il
Center Hotel ££££
A funky boutique hotel
of Bauhaus architecture,
decorated with modern
pieces by local artists. It
also has a great location
by Dizengoff Square.
2 Zamenhof St. Tel: (03)

526 6100. Email:
reservations@atlashotels.
co.il. www.atlas.co.il

Hotel de la Mer ££££

Chic, elegant hotel with
each room decorated on
feng shui principles.
Rooms are bright and
airy with a sea view and
there is a good spa.
*2 Nes Tziona St. Tel: (03)
510 0011.
www.delamer.co.il*

Isrotel Tower ££££

Iconic on the Tel Aviv
skyline is this luxury,
towering, circular hotel
with a rooftop pool –
and a great central
location near the beach.
*78 HaYarkon St. Tel: (03)
511 3636.
www.isrotel.co.il*

EATING OUT

**Abu Hassan (Ali
Karavan) £**

There are three branches
of this place, one of the
city's – and indeed
country's – berst-known
and well-loved hummus
joints.
*1 Dolphin St. Tel: (03)
682 0387. 14 Shivtai
Y'Israel St. Tel: (03) 682
8355. 18 Shivtai Y'Israel
St. Open: Sun–Fri
7.45am–2.45pm.*

**Falafel HaKosem (The
Wizard) £**

The lively wizard himself
dishes up pitta bursting
with falafel, fresh salads
and gooey sauces at this
busy eatery.
*174 HaNevi'im St. Tel:
(03) 525 2033. Open:
Sun–Thur 10am–11pm.*

Hummus Shlomo £

Tucked in behind the
bustling Carmel Market
is this decades-old
hummus joint. Ask
market vendors to point
you in the right
direction.
*Carmel Market. Open:
Sun–Fri 8am–2.30pm.*

Garden Café Sonia ££

Delightful café with a
shady patio garden in
the midst of the city
hubbub. Light meals
are offered.
*1 Almunit Way. Tel: 057
944 2801. Open: daily
9am–midnight.*

Giraffe Noodle Bar ££

Well-priced, quick eats
are offered in this
enormously popular
noodle bar. Sushi, meat
and rice dishes are
also served.
*49 Ibn Gvirol St.
Tel: (03) 691 6294.
Open: daily noon–1am.*

Goocha ££

Fantastic value-for-
money seafood and pasta
restaurant – their
flagship establishment
became so popular that
they opened a second.
The takeaway calamari
and chips is excellent.
*171 Dizengoff St. Tel: (03)
522 2886 & 14 Ibn Gvirol
St. Tel: (03) 691 1603.
Open: daily noon–2am.*

Orna and Ella ££

Light lunches and a
bohemian atmosphere
have made this a long-
standing Sheinkin Street
favourite. Expect queues
at weekends.
*33 Sheinkin St. Tel: (03)
620 4753. Open: Sun–Fri
10am–midnight, Sat
11am–midnight.*

Brasserie £££

Three different menus
are offered throughout
the day at this place
serving French-style
bistro cuisine. Located
on Rabin Square.
*70 Ibn Gvirol St.
Tel: (03) 696 7111.
Open: 24 hours.*

Max Brenner £££

While the mains are
good, it is the
sumptuous, chocolate
desserts that people

come for. Its vast popularity has resulted in branches opening all over the world.

45 Rothschild Boulevard. Tel: (03) 560 4570. www.maxbrenner.com. Open: Sun–Thur 9am–late, Fri & Sat 8am–late.

Cordelia Restaurant ££££

Israeli TV chef Nir Zook has opened a trio of restaurants in Jaffa, and Cordelia is his finest. Housed in an ancient stone building with medieval, romantic décor, it serves French gourmet food.

30 Yeffet St, Jaffa. Tel: (03) 518 4668. Open: Mon–Sat 12.30–3.30pm & 7pm–midnight.

Herbert Samuel ££££

Swanky wine bar and gourmet Mediterranean restaurant on the seafront.

6 Koifman St. Tel: (03) 516 6516. Open: Sun–Wed 12.30pm–12.30am, Thur–Sat 12.30pm–1.30am.

Onami ££££

Well-respected, elegant sushi and Japanese grill.

18 HaArba'a St. Tel: (03)

562 0981. Open: Sun–Fri noon–late, Sat 1pm–late.

Rafael ££££

Rafael is considered one of the top restaurants in Israel and serves a blend of Mediterranean, Moroccan and Middle Eastern dishes.

87 HaYarkon St. Tel: (03) 522 6464. Open: daily noon–3pm & 7pm–late.

ENTERTAINMENT

Barbie

Big venue that hosts the big names of rock.

40 Salame Rd. Tel: (03) 518 8123. Admission varies, depending on performer.

Café Barzilay

Popular, smaller club hosting Israeli and international DJs.

13 HaRachav St. Tel: (03) 687 8090. Open: daily 9pm–late. Admission charge.

Friends

Long-standing Tel Aviv dance bar. Loud music, scantily clad youngsters and plenty of alcohol are on offer.

186 Ben Yehuda St. Tel: 054 803 5757. Open: daily 8pm–late.

HaBima Theatre

Active since 1931, this is the centre of all Jewish and Israeli theatre. It houses a troop of 80 actors who perform regularly (in Hebrew, but English translation is available).

HaBima Square, Tarshat Avenue. Tel: (03) 629 5555. www.habima.co.il

Levontine 7

The Levontine neighbourhood is the new 'in' place in the city, and this bar sums up the atmosphere: relaxed and trendy. Live music nights are often hosted.

7 Levontine St. Tel: (03) 560 5084. Open: daily 7pm–late.

Mann Auditorium

Home to the world-renowned Israeli Philharmonic Orchestra. Tickets can be hard to come by, attesting to its huge popularity.

1 Huberman St. Tel: (03) 621 1777. www.hatarbut.co.il

Rothschild 12

Chic bar designed in a rustic décor on the ever-trendy Rothschild Boulevard.

12 Rothschild Boulevard. Tel: (03) 510 6430. Open: Sat–Thur 7pm–late.

Tel Aviv Cinematheque
Highly respected cinema showing a range of artistic, avant-garde and sensitive-themed films. There is an annual film festival.
Ha'Arba'a St. Tel: (03) 606 0800.
www.cinema.co.il

SPORT AND LEISURE

Bloomfield Stadium
Home to Maccabi Tel Aviv Football Club. Hosts major music concerts and can seat 16,000.
Between HaThiya and She'erit Israel sts. Tel: (02) 625 8844.

Gordon Swimming Pool
Recently renovated saltwater pools, gym and spa.
Gordon Beach. Tel: (03) 762 3300. Open: Sun 1.30–8pm, Mon & Thur 6am–9pm, Tue & Wed 6am–8pm, Fri 6am–7pm, Sat 7am–6pm. Admission charge.

Nokia Arena (Yad Eliyahu Arena)
Home to Maccabi Tel Aviv Basketball Club and the largest indoor arena in the country.
51 Yigal Alon St. Tel: (03) 537 6376.

O-Fun
Bicycle and scooter rental.
197 Ben Yehuda St. Tel: (03) 544 2292. www.rentabikeisrael.com

Sportek
Offers a variety of activities including a trampoline, climbing wall, table tennis and basketball courts.
HaYarkon Park. Tel: (03) 699 0307. www.park.co.il. Admission charge.

Surfpoint
Kite-surfing and windsurfing centre.
Dolphinarium Beach. Tel: 159 956 7888. www.surf-point.co.il. Open: daily 9.30am–dark.

MEDITERRANEAN COAST

Haifa

ACCOMMODATION

Haddad Guest House ££
Family-run guesthouse with a prime location in the German Colony. Excellent value for money.
26 Ben Gurion Avenue. Tel: 772 010 618 (no area code). Email: reservation@haddadguesthouse.com.
www.haddadguesthouse.com

Pundak HaNamal (Port Inn) ££ (dorm £)
Catering to independent budget travellers, this place is located in the port area near downtown. Double rooms and dorms are cosy and comfortable, and facilities include a guest lounge, communal kitchen and garden eating area.
34 Jaffa Rd. Tel: (04) 852 4401. Email: port_inn@yahoo.com. www.portinn.co.il

The Gallery Hotel £££
Understated Bauhaus boutique hotel, with elegant rooms and a well-equipped spa.
61 Herzl St. Tel: (04) 861 6161. Email: gallery@hotelgallery.co.il. www.haifa.hotelgallery.co.il

Colony Hotel ££££
Enjoying a picturesque location in the German Colony, this traditional stone building has classic, elegant décor, big, bright rooms and a café, bar and spa.

28 Ben Gurion Boulevard. Tel: (04) 851 3344. Email: info@colony-hotel.co.il. www.colony-hotel.co.il

Villa Carmel ££££

Small, intimate boutique hotel with classical décor and a great location near Mount Carmel.

1 Heinrich Heine St. Tel: (04) 837 5777. Email: info@villacarmel.co.il. www.villacarmel.co.il

EATING OUT

Abu Shaker £

One of the city's favourite hummus joints.

29 HaMeginim St. Open: daily 6am–6.30pm.

Fatoush £££

With views of the Bahá'í gardens and located in the pretty German Colony, this is a great spot for relaxing in the shady garden with a light meal.

38 Ben Gurion Avenue. Tel: (04) 852 4930. Open: daily 9am–1am.

Jacko Seafood £££

One of the city's best-loved restaurants, Jacko specialises in fish and seafood. It has now opened a second branch.

12 Kehilat Saloniki St & 11 Moriah St. Tel: (04)

810 2355. Open: daily noon–midnight.

Hanamal 24 £££££

Exotic dishes, prime meats and a funky, chic décor have made this the city's trendiest new haunt.

24 HaNamal St. Tel: (04) 862 8899. Open: Mon–Sat noon–midnight.

ENTERTAINMENT

Cinematheque

An arty selection of films is shown daily.

142 HaNassi Avenue. Tel: (04) 835 3530/31. Open: 6–8pm.

Haifa Municipal Theatre

Hebrew theatre performances.

50 Pevsner St. Tel: (04) 860 0555, box office (04) 860 5000.

New Haifa Symphony Orchestra

A well-respected orchestra with sell-out performances.

6 Eliahu Khakim St. Tel: (04) 859 9499. www.haifasymphony.co.il

Pundak HaDov (The Bear)

A chilled-out atmosphere, indoor and outdoor seating areas, hearty pub food and an

extensive cocktail menu.

135 HaNassi Boulevard. Tel: (04) 838 1703. Open: Sun–Fri 11am–late, Fri 6pm–late.

SPORT AND LEISURE

Ze'ev HaYam Diving Club

Offers a range of diving courses and dive packages.

Kishon Port. Tel: (04) 832 3911 & (04) 866 2005. Open: daily 8am–5pm.

Akko

ACCOMMODATION

Akko Gate Hostel ££ (dorms £)

Family-run guesthouse catering to independent budget travellers. Clean, spacious private rooms and dorms available, plus Wi-Fi and a small café. Located right outside the Old City.

14 Saladin St. Tel: (04) 991 0410. Email: walid.akko.gate@gmail. com. www.akkogate.com

Akkotel ££££

Elegant, charming hotel built into the Old City walls. The richly decorated rooms have a range of facilities and there is a wonderful view from the rooftop terrace. *Saladin St. Tel: (04) 987 7100. Email: info@akkotel.com. www.akkotel.com*

Eating out
Humus Saeid ££

Considered one of the country's best hummus joints, it's a tiny restaurant nestled in the souk. Expect to queue. *Market St. Tel: (04) 991 3945. www.humus-saeid.com. Open: Sun–Fri 6am–until the food runs out, around 2.30pm.*

Misedet HaDayagim (The Fisherman's Restaurant) £££

Linked to the fishmonger next door. Simply choose your fish and head into the small, simple eatery where they will fry up your choice and serve it with fresh salads. *Harbour entrance. Tel: (04) 991 1985. Open: daily noon–7pm.*

Uri Buri £££££

Renowned across the country as one of the best fish and seafood restaurants, this unpretentious place serves delicious food in an idyllic spot by the lighthouse. *HaHaganah St. Tel: (04) 955 2212. www.uriburi. co.il. Open: daily noon–midnight.*

Entertainment and leisure
Acco Festival of Alternative Israeli Theatre

Hebrew theatrical productions are performed throughout the festival (a few in English). *www.accofestival.co.il*

Haifa Symphony Orchestra

Performs in the great, echoing Underground Crusader Hall in Akko in July. *www.haifasymphony.co.il*

Ein Hod
Accommodation
ArtRest ££££ (weekday £££)

Imaginative, elegant suites with AC, TV and kitchenettes. Well-tended gardens too. *Tel: (04) 984 1560 & 050 631 0047. Email: arma@netvision.net.il*

Eating out
Café Ein Hod ££

Bohemian and arty, this is the perfect place to enjoy a soya latte, some spicy lentils and the ambience of the village. *Tel: 054 480 1985. Open: Tue–Sun 8.30am–7pm (Thur until late).*

Doña Rosa £££

Cosy Argentinian meat restaurant. *Tel: (04) 954 3777. Open: Mon–Sat 12.30pm–10.30pm.*

Zichron Ya'akov
Accommodation
Achouzat Zamarin £££

Luxurious, unpretentious boutique spa hotel in picturesque Zichron Ya'akov. *16 HaMeyasdim St. Tel: (04) 639 7404. Email: info@zamarin-spa.co.il. www.zamarin-spa.co.il*

Hotel Beit Maimon £££

Offers large, breezy rooms with Jacuzzis that look out on to the Mediterranean Sea. There is a patio for breakfast or coffee with excellent views, and also a small spa.

4 Tzahal St.
Tel: (04) 629 0390.
www.maimon.com

EATING OUT
HaNeshika ££££
Gourmet dining in
an old courtyard
house.
37 HaMeyasdim St.
Tel: (04) 639 0133.
www.haneshika.com.
Open: Mon–Sat
9am–10pm.

Caesarea
ACCOMMODATION
**Dan Caesarea Hotel
£££££**
Considered one of the
best of the Dan chain,
it offers impeccable
service and top-of-the-
range facilities, and
faces both the golf
course and
Mediterranean Sea.
Tel: 170 050 5080.
www.danhotels.com

EATING OUT
**Helena's Archaeological
Park ££££**
Middle Eastern cuisine
served within the
spectacular grounds of
the park.
Tel: (04) 6101018.
Open: daily 12pm–11pm.

**Crusaders
Restaurant £££££**
The menu is varied with
lots of meats and fish,
but the ambience of
eating within the
grounds of the
archaeological park is
the main appeal.
Archaeological Park.
Tel: (04) 6361679. Open:
daily 10am–12am.

SPORT AND LEISURE
Caesarea Dive Club
Part of the archaeological
park, it offers guided or
self-guided underwater
exploration of Herod's
submerged Roman port.
Courses are also available.
Tel: (04) 6265898.
Email: diving@post.com.
www.caesarea-diving.com
Caesarea Golf Club
Israel's only golf course.
Tel: (04) 6109602.

Herzliya
ACCOMMODATION
**Dan Accadia Hotel
£££££**
Part of the Dan chain,
it is perched on the
seafront offering great
views and luxury rooms
and facilities. Sailing,
surfing, scuba diving,
beach volleyball and

countless other active
pursuits can be arranged
at the beach club.
Herzliya Beach.
Tel: (09) 959 7070. Email:
accadia@danhotels.com.
www.danhotels.com
Shizen Spa Resort £££££
Intimate, luxurious hotel,
decked out in Oriental
décor. Rooms are
designed on the
principles of feng shui
and there is a first-rate
spa and Oriental
restaurant.
Herzliya Beach.
Tel: (09) 952 0825.
www.shizenhotel.com

EATING OUT
Moses £££
A long-standing
favourite, it offers hearty
American-style meals in
a relaxed atmosphere.
14 Shenkar St.
Tel: (09) 956 6628.
Open: 12pm–4am daily.
Tapeo ££££
Large, busy restaurant
offering dainty tapas
dishes at reasonable
prices. The ambience
attracts romantic couples
and groups of friends.
9 Shenkar St.
Tel: (09) 954 6699.
Open: 12–2pm &

6pm–1am Sun–Thur,
6pm–1am Fri,
12pm–1am Sat.

Segev ££££

Currently the trendiest
restaurant in town, it has
been decked out in
appearance and
ambience to resemble
Tel Aviv's Neve Tzedek
neighbourhood.
*16 Shenkar St.
Tel: (09) 958 0410.
Open: 12–4pm & 7–11pm
Sun–Thur, 12–3.30pm &
7–11pm Fri, 1–5pm &
7.30–11pm Sat.*

ENTERTAINMENT

Murphy's

This Irish-themed pub is
always busy. You can
expect wooden booths,
running waitresses and
lively music.
*Marina. Tel: (09) 956
9495. Open: 4pm–late
Sun–Thur, 12pm–late
Fri/Sat.*

Yam Bar

Located on the beach,
this is where the
surfers, scuba divers
and students come to
hang out. Grab a beer
and sit on the grass.
*Akadia Beach.
Tel: (09) 959 7102.
Open: 24hrs.*

GALILEE
Nazareth
ACCOMMODATION

Al-Mutran Guesthouse ££ £ (dorm £)

Nestled in the depths
of the cobbled Old
City is this charming,
traditional guesthouse
with a variety of rooms
and dormitories and a
good range of facilities.
*Tel: (04) 645 7947.
Email: info@al-
mutran.com.
www.al-mutran.com*

Fauzi Azar Inn £££ (dorm £)

Enormously popular and
rightly so. Located in the
heart of the Old City in
an ancient courtyard
house, it oozes
traditional charm, has an
excellent range of
facilities and extremely
hospitable owners.
*Tel: (04) 602 0469. Email:
info@fauziazarinn.com.
www.fauziazarinn.com*

St Gabriel Hotel £££

Perched on the cliff
overlooking the city, the
hotel is a beautiful old
building, with big,
pleasant rooms decorated
with Middle Eastern
trappings, and an outside
café with great views.

*2 Salesian St. Tel: (04)
657 2133. Email:
nazsgh@yahoo.com.
www.stgabrielhotel.com*

EATING OUT

Casanova Shawarma £

A small falafel and
shawarma stand with a
selection of fresh salads
to stuff in your pitta.
*Casanova St. Tel: (04) 655
4027. Open: daily
7am–7pm.*

Tishreen ££

A little café set snuggly in
the Old City. This is the
perfect place to drink
Arabic coffee, nibble on
traditional foods
and relax.
*HaMa'ayan Square.
Tel: (04) 608 4666.
Open: Mon–Sat 11am–
midnight, Sun
6pm–midnight.*

Diana £££

Well known across the
country is this
unassuming restaurant
where the food speaks
for itself. The number
and variety of *meze* piled
on your table is mind-
blowing and the meats
are succulent.
*51 Paulus VI St. Tel: (04)
657 2919. Open: daily
11am–midnight.*

Al-Rida £££

Exuding Old Nazareth charm from within an Arab courtyard house, it offers gourmet Middle Eastern dishes.

Al-Bishara St. Tel: (04) 608 4404. Open: Mon–Sat 1pm–2am, Sun 7pm–2am.

SPORT AND LEISURE

Jesus Trail

Guided or self-guided hiking tour from Nazareth to the Sea of Galilee.

Tel: (01 215) 948 2125 (USA). Email: info@jesustrail.com. www.jesustrail.com

Sirin Riders

Horse-riding excursions throughout the Galilee and beyond.

Tel: 052 386 7445. Email: info@ride-israel.com. www.ride-israel.com

Sea of Galilee

ACCOMMODATION

Campsites £

There are camping facilities on all of the Sea of Galilee's beaches. Toilets, showers and barbecue areas are provided.

Sea of Galilee Guesthouse £££

In a small village just off the north shore is this delightful guesthouse offering private rooms with AC and kitchenette, as well as dorms and camping facilities.

Moshav Almagor. Tel: (04) 693 0063. Email: seaofgalileegh@gmail.com

Ein Gev Holiday Resort Village ££££

Located on the Sea of Galilee's prettiest beach, the resort is comprised of guest bungalows spread across green lawns. There is a restaurant, bar and mini market on site.

Ein Gev Beach. Tel: (04) 665 9800. Email: resort@eingev.org.il. www.eingev.com

Vered HaGalil Guest Farm ££££ (weekdays ££)

The farm offers pleasant wood cabins, cottages and suites, all with Jacuzzi, AC and elegant rustic décor.

Route 90 north. Tel: (04) 693 5785. Email: vered@veredhagalil.co.il. www.veredhagalil.com

SPORT AND LEISURE

Vered HaGalil Guest Farm

Offers horse-riding treks, ATV tours and spa.

Route 90 north. Tel: (04) 693 5785. Email: vered@veredhagalil.co.il. www.veredhagalil.com

Tiberias

ACCOMMODATION

Nof HaGalil Hotel (Tiberias Hostel) ££ (dorm £)

Great budget option. While it looks shabby from the outside, inside it has bright, clean private rooms and four-bed dorms (both with AC), a snack bar and bike rental.

Rabin Square. Tel: (04) 679 2611. Email: m11111@012.net.il

Leonardo £££££

Part of the Leonardo chain, this hotel offers a high level of service and comfort, a private beach and swimming pool, and a prime city-centre location.

Gdud Barak St. Tel: (04) 670 0800. Email: reservations.leotib@leonardo-hotels.com. www.leonardo-hotels.com

Scot's Hotel £££££

Originally built as a hospital, it today stands as a beautiful and regal

hotel. The grand stone building has exquisite rooms, sprawling lawns, a gourmet restaurant and tranquil atmosphere. Prices are based on half-board.
1 Gdud Barak St. Tel: (04) 671 0710. Email: scottie@netvision.net.il. www.scotshotels.co.il

EATING OUT
Decks £££
A long-standing Tiberias favourite, unmistakable at the end of a long wooden jetty. It specialises in barbecued and grilled meats and fish. Kosher.
Gdud Barak St. Tel: (04) 672 1538. Open: Sun–Thur 7pm–late, Sat end of Shabbat–late.

Galei Gil ££££
Located right on the promenade, this is a fine place to watch the sunset and enjoy a meal of local St Peter's fish or hearty steak.
Promenade. Tel: (04) 672 0699. Open: daily 11am–midnight.

Scot's Hotel Restaurant £££££
Those looking for gourmet dining in Tiberias will find it in the luxury Scot's Hotel. Magnificent views of the lake, regal décor and an extensive wine list accompany the excellent, albeit pricey, food.
1 Gdud Barak St. Tel: (04) 671 0710. Email: scottie@netvision.net.il. www.scotshotels.co.il

ENTERTAINMENT
Big Ben
Noisy, popular watering hole on the pedestrian walkway. They have a reasonably priced menu of bar snacks too.
Midrahov. Tel: (04) 672 2248. Open: daily noon–late.

Papaya
Dance and cocktail bar on the seafront.
Promenade. Tel: 054 124 1200. Open: daily 5pm–late.

SPORT AND LEISURE
Gai Beach Water Park
Located in the grounds of the Gai Beach Resort Hotel, the water park is a big hit with children and families.
Tel: (04) 670 0713. Open: Passover–Oct 9.30am–5pm. Admission charge.

Tiberias Hot Springs
Seventeen hot springs have given rise to this therapeutic spa centre which offers a plethora of treatments.
Eliezer Kaplan Boulevard. Tel: (04) 672 8580. www.chameytveria.co.il. Open: Sun, Mon & Wed 8am–8pm, Tue & Thur 8am–10pm, Fri & Sat 8am–4pm.

Tiberias Water Sports
Self-drive motorboats, banana boats, waterskiing and lake cruises can all be arranged from here in summer.
Midrahov dock. Tel: 052 269 2664.

Tzfat, Rosh Pina and around
ACCOMMODATION
Horshat Tal Campsite £
Out of the school holiday season, this is one of the nicest places to stay in the region. Cabins or tent pitches are offered amid green lawns and flowing streams.
Horshat Tal National Park. Tel: (04) 694 2360. www.parks.org.il

Safed Inn ££ (dorm £)
The best budget and mid-range option in the north, this family-owned guesthouse offers two-bed dormitories and lovely private rooms. There are also shady gardens, a barbecue area, Internet room and Wi-Fi, cheap laundry and tour booking.
191 Bialik St, Mount Canaan. Tel: (04) 697 1007. Email: leahbb@actcom.net.il. www.safedinn.com

Pina Barosh ££££
Luxury rooms with spectacular views of the northern Galilee are offered at this delightful, plush guesthouse. They also have a covered, outdoor restaurant (*see 'Shiri Bistro' right*).
8 HaHalutzim St, Rosh Pina. Tel: (04) 693 7028. Email: mail@pinabarosh.com. www.pinabarosh.com

Villa Galilee ££££
Stone-built boutique hotel on Mount Canaan. Luxury rooms, a quiet ambience, swimming pool and intimate restaurant.
106 Mount Canaan. Tel: (04) 699 9563. Email: info@villa-galilee.com. www.villa-galilee.com

Mitzpe HaYamim £££££
One of Israel's most luxurious hotels and spas. It has at its core the ideal of healthy living; organic gardens feed the gourmet restaurant (*see 'Muscat Restaurant' below*) and the spa is first rate.
Old Rosh Pina–Tzfat road. Tel: (04) 699 4555. Email: sales@mitzpe-hayamim.com. www.mitzpe-hayamim.com

EATING OUT

Bagdad Café ££
Long-standing favourite with locals and visitors. They serve cheap, light meals.
61 Jerusalem St, Tzfat. Tel: (04) 692 3332. Open: Sun–Thur 8am–10pm.

Café Izidora ££
Set in a leafy little courtyard, they serve light vegetarian meals.
22 Tet Vav St, Tzfat. Tel: 050 886 1564. Open: Sun–Thur 9am–late, Fri 9am–Shabbat.

Mendi's ££
Kosher. And a great place to try some traditional European Jewish dishes.
29 Jerusalem St, Tzfat. Tel: 077 410 8002. Open: Sun–Thur noon–10pm, Fri 9.30am–3 hours before Shabbat.

Gan Eden £££
Comfortable, romantic Italian restaurant offering great views from the top of Mount Canaan.
Mount Canaan. Tel: (04) 697 2434. Open: Sun–Thur 9am–11pm, Fri 9am–2pm.

Shiri Bistro ££££
Part of the guesthouse Pina Barosh (*see left*), the bistro offers a romantic atmosphere and spectacular views across the valley below.
8 HaHalutzim St, Rosh Pina. Tel: (04) 693 7028. Email: mail@pinabarosh.com. www.pinabarosh.com

Muscat Restaurant £££££
Within the Mitzpe HaYamim Hotel (*see above*), Muscat has a creative menu of locally produced foods, and vegetables and food from the hotel's organic garden.
Old Rosh Pina–Tzfat road. Tel: (04) 699 4555. Email: sales@mitzpe-hayamim.com.

www.mitzpe-hayamim.com

ENTERTAINMENT

Blues Brothers Pub

Relaxed, neighbourhood pub with outdoor and indoor areas and chilled music.

Erus St, Rosh Pina. Tel: (04) 693 5336. www.villa-tehila.co.il. Open: Thur–Sat 9pm–late.

SPORT AND LEISURE

Agamon Hula Valley Birdwatching Reserve

Internationally renowned birdwatching site for the north–south migrations. Bicycles, tandems and golf carts can also be rented.

Hula Valley. Tel: (04) 681 7137. www.agamon-hula.co.il. Open: Sun–Thur 9am–1 hour before dusk, Fri & Sat 6.30am–1 hour before dusk. Admission charge.

Canada Centre

Multi-sports centre, including an ice rink, swimming pools and bowling alley.

1 HaRishonim St, Metulla. Tel: (04) 695 037. www.canada-centre.co.il. Open: Mon–Sat 10am–8pm.

Galilee Adventure Park

A cable car leads up to the cliff-top kibbutz and the park offers a fast slide, rappelling, a zipline, a trampoline, bungee dome and climbing wall.

Kibbutz Manara. Tel: (04) 690 5830. www.cliff.co.il. Open: daily 9.30am–4.30pm. Admission charge.

HaGoshrim Kayaks

Busy centre offering kayaking excursions down the Jordan River.

Kibbutz HaGoshrim. Tel: (04) 681 6034. www.kayak.co.il

Kfar Blum Kayaks

Popular kayaking centre offering ziplining and bicycle tours.

Kibbutz Kfar Blum. Tel: (04) 690 2616. www.kayaks.co.il

Golan Heights

ACCOMMODATION

Genghis Khan £

Mongolian tepee dormitories offering unique budget accommodation. Lawns, barbecue areas and plenty of hiking opportunities nearby.

Givat Yo'av. Tel: (052) 371 5687. www.gkhan.co.il

Yehudiya Campsite £

Located by the park offices, it has covered areas for pitching a tent, a bathroom block and barbecue areas. Good for early starts for trips into the park.

Ya'ar Yehudiya National Park. Tel: (04) 696 2817.

Chalet Nimrod Castle £££ (dorm £)

Getting close to nature in the northern Golan Heights is the vibe here, where the hospitable owners offer luxurious eco lodges, dormitories, a campsite and a friendly atmosphere. One of the very few accommodation options in the north.

Nimrod. Tel: (04) 698 4218. Email: biktanimrod@gmail.com. www.bikta.net

Merom Golan Hotel £££

Located in the beautiful kibbutz are these lovely wood cabins and stone hotel, suitable for couples or families.

Kibbutz Merom Golan. Tel: (04) 696 0267. Email: tour_mg@merom-

golan.org.il. www. meromgolantourism.co.il

Ramot Resort Hotel £££ (weekday ££)

Luxurious cabins offer a romantic getaway just outside the village of Ramot. Jacuzzi baths, big-screen TVs, wood floors and manicured grounds.

Entrance to Ramot. Tel: (04) 673 2636. Email: nramot@bezeqint.net. www.ramot-nofesh.co.il

Mitzpe HaShalom Country Lodge ££££ (weekday £££)

The delightful cabins overlooking the Sea of Galilee are well equipped and provide a romantic atmosphere. There is a therapeutic spa experience and breakfast hampers are delivered to your door.

Kfar Haruv. Tel: (04) 676 1767. www.mitzpe-hashalom.co.il

Golan Rooms £££££ (weekday £££)

Bright, sunny cabins with self-catering kitchens, a swimming pool and plenty of tended gardens for lounging around in.

Ramot. Tel: (04) 673 1814. Email: golanrms@ramot-bb.co.il

Hamat Gader Hotel Village £££££

Luxurious, couples hotel within the national park. Each room comes with its own hot-spring pool.

Hamat Gader. Tel: (04) 665 5555. Email: spa-villagehotel@hamat-gader.com. www.spavillage.co.il

EATING OUT

Coffee Anan ££

Located on the summit of Mount Bental, this café is well known as much for its cakes and incredible location as its cheeky name.

Mount Bental. Tel: (04) 682 0664. Open: daily 9am–sunset.

Italkiya b'Ramot ££

Robust, feel-good Italian pastas and pizzas.

Ramot. Tel: 057 944 3778. Open: Mon–Thur 5–10.30pm, Fri & Sat 9am–10.30pm.

Nidal Restaurant ££

While the restaurant looks basic the food is anything but. Great example of Druze dishes and hospitality.

Route 98, Masada. Tel: (04) 698 1066. Open: daily 7.30am–11pm.

HaBokrim Restaurant ££££

Kosher. Rustic meat restaurant that offers a popular weekend buffet.

Kibbutz Merom Golan. Tel: (04) 696 0267. Open: Sun–Thur noon–late, Fri noon–Shabbat.

The Witch's Cauldron and The Milkman ££££

Uniquely popular restaurant that emanates rustic Golan Heights charm served up with hearty cuisine and a cosy ambience.

Nimrod. Tel: (04) 687 0049. Open: daily 10am–late.

Betty and Nachi's Bistro £££££

Offers a unique taster menu of exotic flavours and sumptuous Golan meats.

Ramot. Tel: (04) 673 2889. www.nachi.co.il. Open: Sun, Mon & Wed–Fri 6–11pm.

SPORT AND LEISURE

Bicycle rental

Kibbutz Merom Golan. Tel: (054) 224 7489.

Jeep Point

Specialising in guided jeep tours into the heart of the countryside, this is a big outfit offering a wide range of trips of varying length.

Kibbutz Merom Golan. Tel: (04) 696 3232. Email: perry_s@merom-golan. org.il. www.jeepoint.co.il

Merom Golan Cattleman Ranch

The ranch is located in the centre of the kibbutz and is both a horse-trekking centre and top breeding centre. The horses are healthy and well cared for and there is a high level of safety on the trips.

Kibbutz Merom Golan. Tel: (04) 696 0267.

Merom Golan Quad Bike

Guided quad-bike tours around the region. Guides are experienced and safety regulations good.

Kibbutz Merom Golan. Tel: (04) 696 0483. Email: tractoronim_mg@ walla.com. www.tractoronim.co.il

Ofan Na'im

Bicycle rental.

Ramot. Tel: (04) 673 2524.

Orchan Ramot

Guided jeep tours of the southern Golan Heights. The jeep centre also

offers a nice campsite.

Ramot. Tel: (04) 673 2317. Email: alef1@netvision.net.il. www.orchanramot.co.il

Ramot Horse Ranch

Their horse treks in the surrounding countryside range from a few hours to several days and their animals are well cared for. This is a family-run business that is expanding yearly and will soon offer rural accommodation.

Ramot. Tel: (04) 673 7944. Email: justuri@hotmail.com. www.ramotranch.com

Ski Hermon

The country's only ski resort has had decreasing levels of snow in recent years but can be a fun (but busy) experience when there is good snowfall.

Mount Hermon. Tel: (04) 698 1333. www.skihermon.co.il. Admission charge.

THE SOUTH

Beer Sheva

ACCOMMODATION

Beit Yatziv Hostel ££

Part of the Ilan Ramon science centre. Big,

clean, pleasant rooms have TV and AC, and are very affordable.

79 HaAtzmaut St. Tel: (08) 627 7444. Email: beit_yatziv@ silverbyte.com. www.beityatziv.co.il

Leonardo Negev ££££

Good central location and a wide range of business and visitor facilities, including a swimming pool and restaurant.

4 Henrietta Szold St. Tel: (08) 640 5444. www.leonardo-hotels.com

EATING OUT

Sami Vesusu £££

The best cuts of meats are expertly cooked at the Town Market's most popular eatery.

Town Market, shops 170–180. Tel: (08) 665 2135. Open: Sun–Thur 11am–8.30pm, Fri 10.30am–3.30pm.

Smilansky Tapas Bar £££

Cosy tapas bar in the Old City. Well known and highly regarded around the country.

23 Smilansky St. Tel: (08) 665 4854. Open: Sun–Thur 5pm–2am, Fri & Sat noon–2am.

Yakota 27 £££

Moroccan restaurant serving traditional spiced meaty dishes amid Moroccan décor.
Mordei HaGeta'ot (corner 18 Anilevich St).
Tel: (08) 623 2689.
Open: Sun–Thur noon–midnight, Fri 11am–Shabbat, Sat end Shabbat–midnight.

ENTERTAINMENT
Baraka

One of the city's most popular bar-clubs, it is packed with students during university terms.
70 Shloshet Bnei Harod St. Tel: (08) 628 7111.
Open: daily 10.30pm–late.

Pitput

Trendy bar-restaurant decorated with art from local artists.
122 Herzl St.
Tel: (08) 628 9888.
Open: daily 8.30am– 2am.

SPORT AND LEISURE
Sky Kef Skydiving

Professional skydiving centre located just outside Beer Sheva.
Sde Timan Air Strip.
Tel: 170 070 5867.
Email: info@skykef.com

Sde Boker

ACCOMMODATION
Krivine's Guest House £££ (weekday ££)

Hospitable, family-run guesthouse that is a great budget and mid-range option. Cosy rooms, self-catering kitchen and lots of communal areas and gardens.
Tel: 052 271 2304. Email: guesthouse@krivines.com. www.krivines.com

Boker Valley Vineyard ££££

Wine lodge in the heart of the Negev Desert. Pleasant cabins have a range of in-room facilities, and offer quietness, tranquillity and luxury. They can arrange tours and activities too.
Tel: 052 682 2930.
Email: hilda@kms.org.il.
www.hnbw.net

Carmey Avdat Farm ££££

Vineyard and fruit orchard with luxury cabins built from ecologically sound materials.
Tel: (08) 653 5177.
Email: carmey-avdat@bezeqint.net.
www.carmey-avdat.co.il

Mitzpe Ramon

ACCOMMODATION
Silent Arrow Desert Lodge £

Experience the essence of the desert at this eco lodge. Workshops, meditation and communal living are the appeal.
Tel: 052 661 1561. Email: hetzbasheket@gmail.com. www.silentarrow.co.il

Alpaca Farm £££ (dorm £)

One of the more unusual and surprising desert accommodation options. Private cabins or a communal khan tent are offered, along with many activities (*see p184*).
Tel: (08) 658 8047. Email: alpaca4@gmail.com. www.alpaca.co.il

Isrotel Ramon Inn Hotel ££££

Excellent example of a large chain hotel focusing strongly on green and ecological themes. Luxury rooms, a spa, restaurant and desert activities are offered.
1 Ein Akev St. Tel: (08) 658 8822. Email: info@isrotel.co.il. www.isrotel.co.il

Eating out

HaHavit Restaurant and Café ££

Perched on the edge of the Makhtesh Ramon (Ramon Crater), HaHavit offers spectacular views and decent food.
*Tel: (08) 658 8226.
Open: Sun–Thur 8am–late, Fri 8am–4pm.*

Chez Eugène ££££

Set within the luxury Chez Eugène hotel, this place provides a rare touch of gourmet cuisine in the desert.
*Spice Quarter.
Tel: (08) 653 9595. www.mitzperamonhotel.co.il*

Sport and leisure

Adama Dance Inn

Dance summer camps and workshops. They also have a very nice 70-bed eco lodge.
*Tel: (08) 659 5190. Email: info@adama.org.il.
www.adama.org.il*

Alpaca Farm

Apart from accommodation (*see p183*), this farm offers llama and alpaca feeding, horse-riding trips, wool-weaving workshops and more.

*Tel: (08) 658 8047. Email: alpaca4@gmail.com.
www.alpaca.co.il*

Desert Archery Park

Embark on an archery mission in the middle of the Makhtesh Ramon.
*Tel: 050 534 4598.
www.desertarchery.co.il*

Guide Horizon

Adrenaline-filled buggy tours around the rugged landscape. The tours make stops for coffee and wildlife watching.
*Tel: 052 369 0805. Email: guidmi@netvision.net.il.
www.guidehorizon.com*

Karkom Jeep Tours

Jeep tours are offered by this reputable company that has a good safety record and range of excursions.
*Tel: 052 881 3112. Email: info@negevjeep.co.il.
www.negevjeep.co.il*

Dead Sea

Accommodation

Cycle Inn ££ (dorm £)

Located in a small kibbutz south of the sea is this family-run guesthouse offering cycle tours, private rooms, dormitories and communal kitchen.
Kibbutz Neot HaKikar.

*Tel: (08) 655 2828. Email: esteeuzi@zahav.net.il.
www.cycle-inn.co.il*

Ein Gedi Resort £££

Spacious rooms have AC and TV, and half-board or full-board packages can be arranged with the kibbutz dining room.
*Kibbutz Ein Gedi. Tel: (08) 659 4222. Email: eg@ein-gedi.org.il.
www.ein-gedi.co.il*

Crowne Plaza Dead Sea £££££

Prestigious Dead Sea spa hotel with first-class spa and treatment facilities, luxurious rooms and swimming pools.
*Ein Bokek. Tel: (08) 659 1919. Email: ds_gmsec@hiil.co.il.
www.ichotelsgroup.com*

Daniel Dead Sea Resort & Spa £££££

Equally well equipped but less imposing than some of its neighbours.
*Ein Bokek. Tel: (08) 668 9999.
www.tamareshotels.co.il*

Eating out

Ein Gedi Botanical Garden Restaurant ££

Well-priced buffet with varied Mediterranean-style dishes.

Kibbutz Ein Gedi.
Open: daily 7–9.30am &
noon–2pm & 6–9pm.

Taj Mahal ££££

Delightful place to while
away an evening.
Opulent tents and comfy
cushions are the setting
for eating aromatic
dishes and sipping drinks
into the night.
Located in Tulip-Inn
Hotel, Ein Bokek.
Tel: 057 650 6502.
www.taj-mahal.co.il.
Open: daily noon–sunrise.

SPORT AND LEISURE
Dead Sea Clinic

Specialises in treatments
for a variety of medical
ailments, particularly
those affecting the
skin and respiratory
system.
Central Solarium, Ein
Bokek. Tel: (08) 652 0297.
Email:
deadseaclinic@gmail.com.
www.deadseaclinic.com

Ein Gedi Sea of Spa

Well-equipped spa
and treatment centre
belonging to the
kibbutz.
Tel: (08) 659 4813.
Open: summer 8am–
7pm; winter Sat–Thur
8am–5pm, Fri 8am–4pm.

Arava Desert

ACCOMMODATION

Desert Routes Inn ££
(dorm £)

Located within a small,
isolated moshav, its
private apartments have
AC, TV and kitchenettes
and allow for quiet
appreciation of the desert
surroundings.
Hatzeva. Tel: (08) 658
1829. Email:
shvilimbamidbar@gmail.
com

Desert Ashram £££
(weekday ££ / dorm £)

In the far corner of the
Arava Desert is this zen-
like camp where
meditation, organic meals,
and rooms and cabins
made with ecologically
friendly materials taken
from the desert are offered
as a package.
Shittim. Tel: (08) 632
6508. Email:
ashram@desertashram.co.
il. www.desertashram.co.il

Kibbutz Lotan £££
(dorm £)

Kibbutz Lotan was one
of the pioneers of the eco
kibbutz and offers a
range of meditation
classes and small but
cosy cabins made from
materials such as wood,

mud and straw sourced
sustainably from the
desert region.
Tel: (08) 635 6935. Email:
lotan-programs@
lotan.ardom.co.il.
www.kibbutzlotan.com

Negev Eco Lodge £££
(dorm £)

Ecologically sound
materials were used to
create desert
accommodation and a
natural experience. There
is a khan tent dormitory,
swimming pool and
relaxed communal
atmosphere.
Zuqim. Tel: 052 617 0028.
Email: desert-
days@arava.co.il.
www.desert-days.co.il

EATING OUT
Ne'ot Smadar £££

Organic café, restaurant
and shop in the heart of
the desert.
Ketura Junction. Tel: (08)
635 8111. Open: Sun–
Thur 6am–9pm, Fri 6am–
3pm, Sat 6–9pm.

SPORT AND LEISURE
Camel Riders

Treks into the remote
desert, with stays in
Bedouin camps and
traditional food cooked

in the open air.
Shaharut. Tel: (08) 637 3218. www.camel-riders.com

Kibbutz Lotan

One of the pioneers of the desert eco trend, the kibbutz offers holistic therapies and workshops, as well as cabins made from environmentally friendly materials (*see p185*).
Tel: (08) 635 6935. Email: lotan-programs@ lotan.ardom.co.il. www.kibbutzlotan.com

Eilat

ACCOMMODATION

Hotel Pierre £

Excellent budget and mid-range option for those wanting to avoid hostels. Rooms are simple but have TV and AC.
123 Retamim St. Tel: (07) 632 6601. Email: pierrehotel@bezeqint.net. www.eilat-guide. com/pierre

Arava Hostel ££ (dorm £)

Long-standing Eilat hostel offering private rooms with AC or clean, tidy dormitories. Facilities include Internet access, a communal

kitchen, and barbecue and outdoor eating area.
106 Almogim St. Tel: (08) 637 4687. Email: harava@bezeqint.net. www.a55.co.il

Hilton Queen of Sheba Hotel £££££

One of the Middle East's most prestigious, flamboyant and plush hotels.
8 Antibes St. Tel: (08) 630 6666. www.hilton.com

The Orchid Hotel and Resort £££££

Understated, elegant hotel on the southern beach. Tropical pools and lush gardens surround the luxurious rooms and there is a spa and high-end Thai restaurant.
South Beach. Tel: (08) 636 0360. www.orchidhotel.co.il

EATING OUT

Duda Restaurant ££

Good, cheap hummus, salads and chips.
Dahlia Hotel, North Beach. Tel: (08) 633 0389. Open: 24 hours.

Pastory £££

Nourishing Italian pasta dishes, meats and home-made ice-cream.
7 Tarshish St. Tel: (08)

634 5111. Open: daily 1pm–11pm.

Pasador ££££

Unassuming, chic décor and a varied set menu.
Americana Hotel, 10 Kaman St. Tel: (08) 637 8228. Open: daily 12.30pm–midnight.

Caso do Brasil £££££

Brazilian meat house considered one of the best restaurants in the city. Price is based on all-you-can-eat.
3 Hativat Golani St. Tel: (08) 632 3032. www. casadobrasil.co.il. Open: daily noon–midnight.

ENTERTAINMENT

Dolphin Reef Pub

Enjoy a relaxed beer with the dolphins jumping in the background.
Dolphin Reef, South Beach. Open: when the park closes.

IMAX 3-D

Regular showings of 3-D films.
4 Yotam Rd. Tel: (08) 636 1000. Email: marka@imaxeilat.co.il. www.imaxeilat.co.il. Open: Sun–Thur 11am–midnight, Fri 11am–Shabbat, Sat 9pm–1am. Admission charge.

King's City

Popular with children is this biblical-themed amusement park.

Opposite New Lagoon. Tel: (08) 630 4444. Email: sales3@kingscity.co.il. www.kingscity.co.il. Open: Sun–Thur 9am–1am, Fri 9am–Shabbat, Sat end of Shabbat–1am. Admission charge.

Paddy's Irish Bar

Great place for some imported beers and live televised sporting events.

New Tourist Centre building. Tel: (08) 637 0921. Open: daily noon–4am.

The Three Monkeys

Long-standing, popular beachfront bar.

North Beach. Tel: (08) 636 8800. Open: daily 9pm–3am.

SPORT AND LEISURE

Aqua Sport

Scuba-diving centre offering courses, guided dives and dive tours to Egypt and Jordan.

Coral Beach. Tel: (08) 633 4404. Email: info@aqua-sport.com. www.aqua-sport.com

International Birding and Research Centre

Birdwatching centre for flocks migrating north and south.

Tel: 050 211 2498. Email: ibrce@eilatcity.co.il.

www.birdsofeilat.com

Rcd Sea Sports

Scuba and watersports centre. Watersports operate from Jetty C on the King Solomon's Wharf in town, while the scuba centre is located on Coral Beach.

Coral Beach, Ambassador Hotel. Tel: (08) 633 3666. www.redseasports.co.il

Siam Divers

Big, fabulously well-equipped scuba centre offering courses, as well as dive excursions to Sinai and Aqaba.

Coral Beach. Tel: (08) 632 3636. Email: info@deepdivers.co.il. www.siam.co.il

Index

Acknowledgements

Thomas Cook Publishing wishes to thank MARK BASSETT, to whom the copyright belongs, for the photographs in this book, except for the following images:

Alamy 105
Dreamstime (Ryan Beiler) 165
Israel GTO 1, 5, 9, 11, 23, 25, 27, 28, 36, 38, 39, 41, 42, 43, 45, 46, 47, 48, 51, 63, 64, 73, 76, 94, 109, 111, 112, 113, 117, 124, 125, 134, 150, 159
iTravelJerusalem 77, 108, 133
Pictures Colour Library 141, 147

For CAMBRIDGE PUBLISHING MANAGEMENT LIMITED:
Project editors: Jennifer Jahn & Thomas Willsher
Copy editor: Anne McGregor
Typesetter: Paul Queripel
Proofreaders: Caroline Hunt & Cath Senker
Indexer: Marie Lorimer

SEND YOUR THOUGHTS TO
BOOKS@THOMASCOOK.COM

We're committed to providing the very best up-to-date information in our travel guides and constantly strive to make them as useful as they can be. You can help us to improve future editions by letting us have your feedback. If you've made a wonderful discovery on your travels that we don't already feature, if you'd like to inform us about recent changes to anything that we do include, or if you simply want to let us know your thoughts about this guidebook and how we can make it even better – we'd love to hear from you.

Send us ideas, discoveries and recommendations today and then look out for your valuable input in the next edition of this title.

Emails to the above address, or letters to the traveller guides Series Editor, Thomas Cook Publishing, PO Box 227, Coningsby Road, Peterborough PE3 8SB, UK.

Please don't forget to let us know which title your feedback refers to!